concrete
countertops
made simple

concrete countertops madesimple

A step-by-step guide

Fu-Tung Cheng

Photography by Matthew Millman

The Taunton Press

To Mom Sung Yuan Cheng, again and again

 The Taunton Press

The Taunton Press, Inc., 63 South Main Street, PO Box 5506, Newtown, CT 06470-5506
e-mail: tp@taunton.com

Editor: Steve Culpepper
Jacket/Cover design: Loop Design, Jason Carreiro
Copy editor: Candace B. Levy
Indexer: Catherine Goddard
Interior design: Carol Petro, Chika Azuma
Layout: Carol Petro
Illustrator: Mario Ferro
Photographer: All photography by Matthew Millman unless otherwise noted.
DVD: Todd Osborn

Library of Congress Cataloging-in-Publication Data
Cheng, Fu-Tung.
 Concrete countertops made simple : a step-by-step guide / Fu-Tung Cheng ; photographer, Matthew Millman.
    p. cm.
 Includes bibliographical references and index.
 ISBN 978-1-56158-882-4 (alk. paper)
 1. Concrete countertops--Design and construction. 2. Concrete construction--Formwork. 3. Countertops--Materials. I. Title.
 TT197.5.C68C4925 2008
 624.1'834--dc22
                    2008022508

Printed in the United States of America
10 9 8 7 6 5 4 3 2 1

The following manufacturers/names appearing in *Concrete Countertops Made Simple* are trademarks: Alpha Professional Tools®, Basalite®, Bungee®, *Concrete Decor*™ magazine, Contractors Direct℠, Formica®, Ideal Tile℠ Kitchen & Bath Design Center, Imer USA, Inc.®, Interstar®, Makita®, Masonite®, Melamine®, Mylar®, PC-7®, Phillips®, Plexiglas®, Polytek Development Corporation®, Sakrete®, Sharpie®, Smooth-On®, Speed® Square, Tapcon®, Velcro®, Vibco®.

Construction is inherently dangerous. Using hand or power tools improperly or ignoring safety practices can lead to permanent injury or even death. Don't try to perform operations you learn about here (or elsewhere) unless you're certain they are safe for you. If something about an operation doesn't feel right, don't do it. Look for another way. We want you to enjoy the craft, so please keep safety foremost in your mind whenever you're in the shop.

acknowledgments

Much gratitude to Todd Osborn, videographer, for his friendship and commitment to quality; Matt Millman, longtime collaborator, photographer, and now plumber extraordinaire; Clay Lai, who crafted the perfect set; and Mike Heidebrink, a partner, for great ideas, steadfastness, and equanimity.

Also thanks to Ann Kim, architect, for designing around the impossible without complaint; Steve Culpepper, Taunton's executive editor, for tolerance and forbearance of me, his recurring nightmare, and the wisdom of introducing me to Scott Gibson, writer and author, who so adroitly danced my text around that I couldn't tell his voice from mine. And thanks to my wife, Lila Luk, for hanging in the balance, and to my daughter, An-Ya Cheng, for climbing aboard Cat Bus for the wild ride to the bathroom each morning.

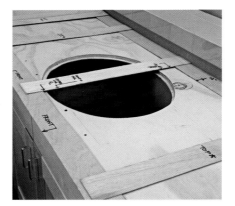

contents

preface

I made my first concrete countertop as a do-it-myself project for my own kitchen in 1985. Thousands of meals later, my family still uses it every day. We love it, and so does everyone else who sees it.

My goal back then was simple: to create something special and save money. Little did I realize that affluent homeowners would someday covet countertops made of concrete. Or that my first book, *Concrete Countertops: Design, Forms, and Finishes for the New Kitchen and Bath,* would encourage so many artisans to make concrete counters for the luxury market that soon developed. But the biggest surprise was that there were so many fearless homeowners willing to make countertops for themselves.

Many people find the cost of a professional, custom countertop too much for their remodeled kitchens. *Concrete Countertops Made Simple* is my attempt to resolve this dilemma by helping homeowners create their own counters that are affordable, green, and unique. With this book, making concrete countertops comes full circle, back to its origins as a creative do-it-yourself project that's a lot of fun and very satisfying.

Take your time and follow the instructions, and you will get it right the first time. If you're not sure you want to jump into a full-size kitchen counter, you can start modestly with the bathroom vanity countertop we demonstrate in this book.

What's fun about concrete countertops is that anyone can make one: from the amateur with the simplest of tools to the expert who has a fully equipped shop.

This kind of project is more akin to cooking than to building—and it's no accident there are lots of references to cooking throughout this book. Cooking got me started designing my kitchen in the first place. If it weren't for that, I'd probably still be buttering my toast on a Formica® countertop.

When you first take an interest in cooking, you're probably not ready to tackle a 10-course Italian banquet. But it's satisfying to prepare your own version of a family recipe and serve it up to friends. That's the same sense of personal satisfaction and creative gratification that you get when making your first concrete countertop.

Think of cement, sand, and rock as though they were flour, baking powder, and salt. Add water to the right blend of dry ingredients, and you get concrete batter. Countertop making is like baking an upside-down cake in a wooden pan. You simply mix and pour the concrete batter into the smooth mold. You even get to stick your fingers in the batter (but no licking!). Your hands get dirty; it's a bit of a mess. You let it bake (no oven required). In 4 days to 5 days, pop it out of the mold and (with some beefy help) turn it over. To finish it out, you polish the already flat surface with a hand polisher and seal it.

The process is fun and affordable. Using the instructions in this book, you should be able to complete a counter in about two weekends. Not only will the result be as beautiful as anything you could buy but you will have created it yourself. You won't be able to keep your hands off of it, and neither will anyone else who sees it.

Why use concrete?

Though many people still think of concrete as being used for foundations and sidewalks, this amazing material is now commonly found in kitchens and bathrooms—in the form of concrete countertops.

Sure, we're still more accustomed to granite, stone composites, stainless steel, plastic laminates, and solid surfacing. And those can be great materials for your countertop. But once you see and feel the timeless, earthy appeal of concrete, you'll wonder why it isn't used for many more counters.

When you make a concrete countertop with your own hands, you are doing yourself and the earth a small favor. It's greener, more affordable, potentially healthier, and a lot more fun than buying monotonous granite countertops that are mined, fabricated, and shipped by boat from faraway countries. Other countertop choices, such as stone composites, are manufactured in factories from mineral particles and epoxies and trucked hundreds of miles to a fabrication shop, and then, finally, to you.

Nothing is wrong with those other countertop materials. Each has benefits and limitations. In fact, combinations of dissimilar materials can make them more interesting while spicing up what can be a relentlessly uniform array of surfaces. But, by making your own concrete countertop, you have fun, create something unique, save lots of money, and shrink your carbon footprint to boot.

A drain board of inlaid slate tile and a perforated stainless-steel soap tray combine form and function with concrete.

Concrete is the "earthy" accent countertop (at right) that complements the main stainless-steel sink counter.

Concrete characteristics

There's a lot to like about concrete. It conveys the solid mass of rock. It feels real, not machine made. You can inlay objects into the surface, and you can shape concrete into appealing curves. It feels warm, comfortable, and natural—not too slick and glossy, not too soft, and certainly not at all like plastic.

Concrete counters are easy to personalize. Embed just about anything you like in the surface: mementos, minerals, metal parts, fossils, tiles, mosaics, car parts, computer chips—you name it. After a light polish of the cured concrete, there they are.

The two-piece concrete countertop and concrete wall combine with an inlaid marble baking board.

WHY NOT POUR IN PLACE?

Why not simply build your concrete countertop form on top of the existing cabinet, pour in the concrete, and call it a day?

At first glance, it seems to be the fastest, easiest way to go, especially for the DIYer: Remove the old countertop, put edges around your existing cabinets, pour in the mix, trowel it smooth, and you're done.

However, a cured countertop must be absolutely flat before it can be polished. In the hands of the inexperienced, troweling results in surface irregularities that require time and skill to grind flat and to polish. That's the reason many unpolished, poured-in-place countertops look rustic and slightly crude.

With a mold, the flat, finished surface of the countertop is on the bottom of the pour. Because the mold material, Melamine®, is dead flat and the table or platform we are pouring on is flat and level, it's the mold that does the work. After the pour, when the cured countertop is removed from the mold and turned over, the surface is automatically flat. And when there are no uneven surfaces to deal with, polishing is easy.

Finally, with the poured-in-place method, even master finishers can't match the detail possible with the mold process. It is virtually impossible to tool in fine details such as edges, drain boards, soap dishes, and shelves.

Strengths and weaknesses

Concrete in combination with embedded rebar (reinforcing steel bar) can support itself, span distance, and cantilever over space. This unique property of reinforced concrete frees the countertop to "float" over areas without support and allows for maximum creative expression. Locating the position of the rebar within the countertop depends on what "work" is done. When in doubt about structural integrity, consult an engineer.

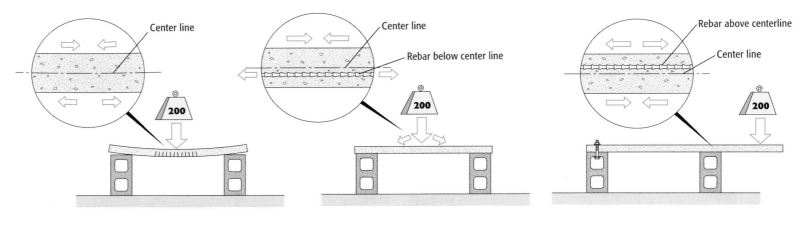

No rebar   Rebar span   Rebar cantilever

Too often bathroom and kitchen countertops are the same unimaginative slabs plopped atop cabinet boxes. I call this look "box-and-slab design." Counters are always ¾-in. slabs made up to appear 1½ in. thick by building up the edges.

It doesn't have to be that way. One of the beauties of concrete is that it can be cast in just about any thickness you want. I usually make concrete countertops at least 2½ in. thick, giving them a mass and presence that a standard counter just doesn't have. Carry these techniques into more elaborate designs and you can make countertops in which different sections are made in different thicknesses. Think of the possibilities.

Pros and cons

For all of its many advantages as a countertop material, concrete has a few disadvantages. It's sort of like having a wood floor in your home. Wood certainly isn't the most trouble-free material you could choose: It can be scuffed, dented, and stained. Under some circumstances, it will crack or split. Unsealed and exposed to moisture, wood floors warp and discolor. But people still love wood floors because they bring a warmth into the home and because the flaws that wood floors inevitably develop over time add unique character.

Concrete, however, is far more durable than wood. Look at the Roman aqueducts. Made of concrete thousands of years ago, they're still standing, and some are still in use.

The following are some problems you could experience, though most can be avoided if you follow the instructions in this book.

Cracks Concrete occasionally can develop hairline cracks over time. Cracking can be largely controlled by using the right blend of additives in the concrete mix and by embedding steel to strengthen it. Most problems with cracks are caused by a poor cement mix and improper curing. But there is no absolute guarantee that tiny cracks will be completely eliminated. And although it is extremely durable, the surface of a concrete counter can be scratched much the way that marble can.

Continued on page 12

Concrete can be shaped and inset to allow for accessories such as this perforated stainless-steel shelf.

With rebar, concrete can span and hold itself rigid—as with this simple entry shelf.

A dropped edge with two lengths of rebar enables this countertop to cover a 7-ft. span. (Photo Fu-Tung Cheng)

Simple and solid: a steel leg supports a 4-ft. breakfast bar in this 1950s Eichler home.

Concrete's plastic qualities make it an ideal material for forming into any shape you like. It doesn't have to be a simple rectangle with square edges.

Finishing touches such as polished stone inlaid into the concrete countertop personalize your kitchen.

These Pro-Formula admixture color samples are made of iron oxides (a form of rust) or other natural minerals. Notice how the hue and intensity of the colors change depending on how much of the aggregates are exposed through the polishing process.

Continued from page 8

Staining Unsealed, concrete is vulnerable to acid etching and oil stains. Wine, lemon juice, vinegar, soft drinks, and vegetable oil leave unsightly marks on an unprotected concrete countertop. Once it is sealed, concrete performs well, but it needs periodic maintenance. You can use either a topical sealer or a penetrating sealer. In either case, sealers must be waxed from time to time to prevent wear. Wines, citrus juice, vinegar, and oil must be wiped up within hours. Otherwise they can slowly etch their way through the sealer and will eventually blemish the surface of the countertop.

Weight Concrete is heavy; there's no getting around that. Well-built cabinets can handle this weight without any special reinforcements, although you should take a careful look to see how your cabinet is built and reinforce if necessary (see "Beefing up a cabinet" on p. 93). Concrete's weight will also be a factor as you make the counter. You'll need a sturdy work surface, and you'll need some help when it comes time to pop the counter out of the mold and install it.

Why do-it-yourself?

It's green When you buy inexpensive sacked concrete for your countertop from your neighborhood home improvement center, it's made from regionally made cement and locally quarried common rocks and sand. This not only minimizes transportation costs but also helps your community's economy. Thinking globally and shopping locally lessens the amount of energy we consume.

Save money You save considerable money by making a concrete countertop yourself because the material costs are so low. Sacks of concrete, plywood, Melamine sheets, and sawhorses are all common, inexpensive building materials, readily available just around the corner from your house. Admixtures to bolster concrete to countertop-grade strength are available on-line. A common cement mixer, a vibrator, and a hand polisher are all the equipment you'll need. They can be rented by the day at a reasonable rate at any local tool rental yard.

It's creative You get to add creative touches with recycled glass, shells, garage sale finds, and personal mementos.

What is concrete?

Concrete has an extremely long history. During the Bronze Age, Greeks concocted a blend of volcanic ash, lime, and sand to make mortar. Portland cement—the key component of modern concrete—was invented by an English bricklayer in 1824. The material has steadily improved since then but remains fundamentally the same. Today, several types of portland cement are commonly available, each with different attributes.

At its most basic, concrete is a mixture of portland cement, sand, and crushed stone or gravel (*coarse aggregates*). But a variety of additives (called *admixtures*) such as water reducers, pigments, and reinforcing fibers are blended into the mix to modify its properties for countertops.

While professional chefs often make cake using flour, eggs, salt, butter, and other raw ingredients, many amateur cooks prefer the convenience of packaged, ready-made cake mix. Similarly, a concrete countertop professional might start with cement powder, weighing out the correct proportions of rock and sand and then adding all sorts of additives. This kind of from-scratch custom mixing is tedious and beyond the scope of this book. We start with the common bagged concrete you can buy in just about any hardware or building supply stores. Then we simply add convenient, ready-made, packaged admixtures made specifically for concrete countertops (see Resources on p. 102).

The right stuff

Portland cement starts as lime or calcium carbonate, which is mixed with silica and iron oxides and heated at high temperatures in huge ovens. This produces rock-hard nuggets that are ground into a fine powder to become portland cement. Type I is the most common kind of cement, but it's more susceptible to shrinking and cracking than type II or type III cement; those would make a better choice for counters if you were making your own concrete from scratch.

Cakes are made from common, readily available ingredients combined in just the right way . . .

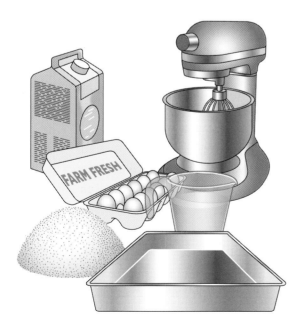

. . . and so are concrete countertops.

Premixed concrete comes in 60-lb. and 80-lb. sacks. If we were making cakes, this would be our flour. Generally, two types of bagged concrete are available: *Ordinary concrete* rated at 2,500 pounds per square inch (psi) to 2,800 psi; *high-strength concrete* rated at 4,000 psi to 5,000 psi.

These ratings are a measure of hardness. Higher-strength, 5,000-psi mix has more cement content in each sack. It is used for jobs that require the concrete to support heavy loads, where quality control matters. In my shop, I start with Sakrete® 5000 and mix in Pro-Formula admixture to make a professional-grade countertop. High-strength varieties are usually available in the same retail outlets as standard concrete mix and cost only slightly more. It's well worth the small added expense.

The tools you'll need

Like any home-improvement project, you'll need a variety of tools. Some you may already have; others are specialty tools, often expensive, that you may want to borrow (if you're lucky enough to have a contractor for a best friend) or rent. Before you start on your concrete countertop project, get all the tools and materials you'll need and have them ready when you need them.

Must-have tools

You will need some basic hand and power tools that, with one exception, aren't very expensive. If you're adventuresome enough to build your own concrete countertop, you probably have them on hand already.

- Drill/driver for driving screws
- Hot-glue gun
- Felt-tipped marker
- Speed® Square (a carpenter's layout tool available in most hardware stores and lumberyards)
- Measuring tape
- Blue painter's masking tape
- Framing square

If you don't have a tablesaw for cutting parts for the mold, consider adding a portable model to your need-to-rent list or borrow one from that contractor friend. Sheets of plywood and Melamine, which are used to make the template and the mold for the counter, must be cut into precise pieces—a job best left to a tablesaw. If you have a circular saw and an accurate guide, you may be able to do without the tablesaw. Alternately, you can try the amazing new no-tool foam mold technique (see Chapter 2).

Rent the big-ticket items

Some of the tools you'll need for mixing, pouring, and finishing the concrete are expensive, so unless you imagine needing them on a regular basis you're better off renting. Any well-stocked rental center should be able to supply the ones discussed here.

Mixer An electric- or gas-powered mixer thoroughly combines all of the ingredients with a lot less effort and with better results than mixing the concrete in a wheelbarrow with a shovel or hoe. When renting a mixer, here's something to remember: Rented mixers typically have a maximum rated capacity of 9 cu. ft., though they actually hold only about 5 cu. ft. of concrete. A concrete counter of about 12 sq. ft. and 3 in. thick will contain about 4 cu. ft. of concrete.

Vibrator After the concrete has been placed in the mold, it should be vibrated, a process that liquefies the mix so it flows into every nook and cranny and removes trapped air that would lead to pits in the finished surface. There really is no substitute for a professional concrete vibrator, called a *stinger*. They are available at most rental yards or on-line. For our purposes, the smaller stingers, with heads of less than 1 in. in diameter, are best, and they come in corded and cordless versions.

Variable-speed polisher After the countertop has been popped out of its mold, it should be polished. In my shop, I use an Alpha polisher that's adjustable from 900 rpm to 2,700 rpm. It has a water feed that keeps the surface wet as you work. It accepts 5-in. Velcro®-backed diamond abrasive pads, making pad changes very simple. Any polisher you can rent with these features will make the work go more easily. There is a worthy, everyday substitute for this professional type polisher: an ordinary orbital sander with a Velcro pad. It won't polish as aggressively as a pro tool, so expect the polishing process to take more time. For the water feed, take a 1-qt. plastic food container and poke a few small holes at the bottom, fill with water, and—voilà!—a water feed. **Important:** *Make sure your orbital sander is double-insulated, and use it with a ground fault circuit interrupter (GFCI) on a grounded outlet. Otherwise you risk severe electric shock.*

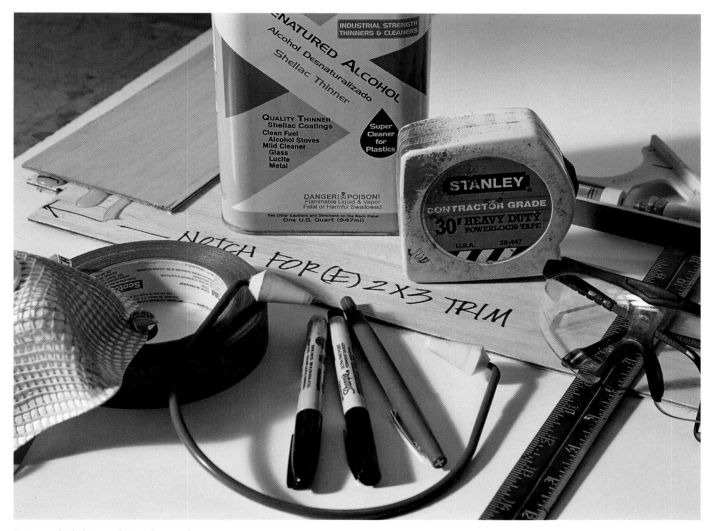

Be sure to include a mask, ear plugs, and safety glasses as part of the basic equipment you'll need.

Cheng Design. Olsen kitchen, El Cerrito, CA.
(Photo Matthew Millman)

What you can accomplish

Since my first book, *Concrete Countertops,* came out in 2002, homeowners and contractors all over the country have sent me photographs of the projects they have built. As you can see, many are quite elaborate and creative. I've also included a few of my own designs. Although I show you how to build a very basic concrete countertop in this book, what you do with the information is limited only by your imagination and your ambition.

Cheng Design. Benchtop, San Francisco. (Photo Tim Maloney)

An advanced workshop taught by the author.

Absolute Concrete Works. Bainbridge Island, WA. (Photo Northlight Photography)

Keelin Kennedy, Barefoot Design. Chicago.
(Photos Scott Shigley Photography)

Cheng Design.
Soapdish detail.
(Photo Tim Maloney)

Jamie McGuire, Lokahi Stone. Oahu, HI.
(Photo Ric Noyle Photography)

Cheng Design. Inlay detail.
(Photo Tim Maloney)

Jamie McGuire, Lokahi Stone. Oahu, HI.
(Photo Ric Noyle Photography)

Chris Jarman, Concrete Connection. Farmhouse kitchen, Oak Hill, VA. (Photo Chris Jarman)

Chris Coyne, Bighorn Architectural Concrete. Bath surround, Southwest Montana. (Photo Brad Baumann)

Cheng Design. Sebastopol, CA. (Photo Fu-Tung Cheng)

Making a template

**L**arge concrete countertops can be as complex as you want to make them. Cast in two or more pieces, they can incorporate integral drain boards, include elaborate sculptural inlays, and be molded into a variety of interwoven contours and shapes. Once you're comfortable with the basic vanity countertop recipe shown in this book you can try your hand with molds with more features. That's all part of the fun of working with concrete.

We're choosing to start with a simple rectangular countertop for a bathroom vanity, a satisfying project in its own right, with plenty of opportunities for adding details to make it uniquely your own. It's also an excellent way of learning the basics.

This countertop can be made over the course of two weekends. The result will be something you'll love to use and show off for years to come.

⅛-in. lauan plywood is easily ripped into 3-in. strips for the template on a small, portable tablesaw.

The basics of template making

There's a simple reason why you can't make a mold for a new counter by just measuring the length and depth of the cabinet—the completed counter probably wouldn't fit. Even in a new house, corners are often out of square or some other irregularity creeps in.

That's why a concrete countertop begins with a template. It's a precise, full-scale map of the project. The template becomes the outline for a mold that will be used to form the concrete. The template also is the place to record important information about the countertop and serves as a way of recognizing potential problems before they're cast in stone.

I make templates by hot-gluing together strips of ⅛-in.-thick lauan plywood (sometimes called "door skin"), which is inexpensive and readily available. (Strips of posterboard can also work.) Start by cutting strips 3 in. wide and the full 8-ft. length of the sheet, with either a tablesaw or a circular saw and a guide. The edges of the strips should be straight and parallel.

The tools you'll need for the template and making the sink knockout are for measuring, marking, and laying out the plan for your countertop and so include a tape and two kinds of squares, a handheld jigsaw, a glue gun, lightweight strips of lauan plywood (or "door skin"), and material for the knockouts (such as polystyrene foam).

TOOLS AND MATERIALS

- Tablesaw or circular saw to cut the sheets of lauan into strips

- Drill to bore access holes into the plywood substrate

- Glue gun with all-purpose glue sticks for fastening together the pieces of the light wood template

- Framing square to check for how square (90 degree angle) the existing cabinet base and room corners are

- Speed Square, or combination square, for measuring overhang and depth

- Tape measure for measuring dimensions

- Electric jigsaw, or fine-tooth Japanese-style handsaw, for cutting the poly– styrene foam

- Sharpie® marker to make indelible and easy-to-read marks and notations on the template

- Lauan door skin strips (or strips of stiff poster board) to create the basic template

- Ready-made rubber faucet and sink knockouts or material to make them, such as disks of foam or plywood

- Extruded polystyrene board (rigid-foam insulation) for the sink knockout, either stacked to the appropriate depth or cut from a piece of the correct thickness

- Fine sandpaper for smoothing the foam sink knockout

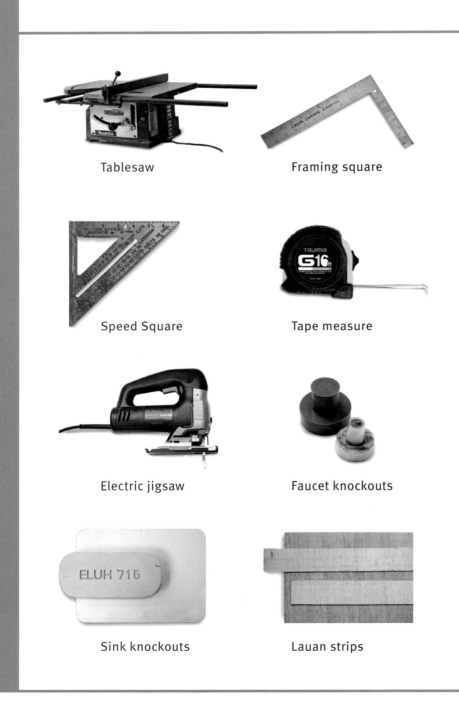

Tablesaw

Framing square

Speed Square

Tape measure

Electric jigsaw

Faucet knockouts

Sink knockouts

Lauan strips

Supporting the weight

A piece of ¾-in. plywood can be added to the top of the cabinet box for additional support. It can be finished with veneer or metal to hide the raw edge. Built this way, the finished counter will be 1¾ in. higher than standard.

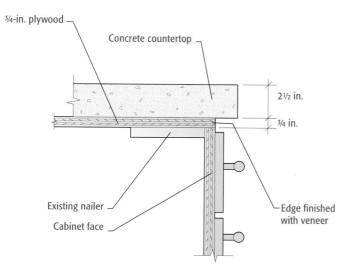

¾-in. plywood

Concrete countertop

2½ in.

¾ in.

Existing nailer

Cabinet face

Edge finished with veneer

Visual substance

You're about to make the template for your concrete countertop, which takes into account thickness and depth, or overhang. It's important to consider the final size of the countertop when you're making a template.

Thickness and overhang

The front edges of conventional countertops are usually built up to appear 1½ in. thick. I like concrete countertops to be at least 2½ in. thick—a dimension that emphasizes the inherent strength of concrete. Also, at a minimum, the front edge of the counter should extend to a point in line with the front of the drawer faces or pulls. So factor that in as you make the template.

An undermount sink shows off the thickness of the countertop and reinforces the feel of the mass and solidity of concrete.

Details

A recessed soap dish and inlays of found objects are easy to add, and they make a countertop unique. Your sense of design, your choice of details, your use of color and shapes will make the countertop distinctively yours.

Our project countertop: a 26-in. by 60-in. vanity with integral soap dish. Notice the gradation of the concrete surface from fine to course aggregates.

Make the template

1 Measure and cut Carefully measure the length and depth of the cabinet where the counter will be installed, factoring in the overhang, and trim the strips of lauan so they are ½ in. shorter than those dimensions. A Speed Square butted against the drawer front allows you to stabilize the tape measure to ensure an accurate measurement.

2 Start placing strips Now place one long strip along the back edge of the counter and a second long strip across the front edge, bringing the edge of the front strip beyond the cabinet front to create the overhang. Then cut the shorter strips that will run front to back, and rest them in place. Remember that the shorter strips are also ½ in. or so shorter than the actual depth of the counter.

3 Secure with hot glue The strips marking the depth of the counter should overlap the long strips at the front and back. With the strips that butt the walls tight against the walls, you will have an accurate representation of the countertop dimensions. Mark all locations with a Sharpie before removing the short strips one at a time and applying a bead of hot-melt glue to the lauan beneath. Check that each strip is lined up with your marks, and press it back in place. Hold each glue joint until the glue sets, which takes about 30 seconds.

4 Mark knockouts Next, mark the location of the sink knockout and faucet knockouts on the lauan; then place the sink knockout on top of the template, and line up the centerlines with the marks on the template to determine the location of the sink. (Now's a good time to break out your digital camera and take a photo of the template. Later, the photo will give you an easy reference for what you've done so far.)

This cabinet needed reinforcement, so a ¾-in. plywood substrate was added to the top to provide extra strength.

Where your countertop begins

At this point I've already created a rough drawing of my countertop and cut the thin strips of lauan that I'll glue together to make my template. And I have all the other stuff I'll need within reach. For the project I'm doing here, I added ¾-in. thick plywood to the top of the vanity to support the new countertop (that plywood layer is called a *substrate*). I also cut a sink opening in the substrate and tooled a groove around the edge of the opening so the top of the sink will sit flush with the plywood (see the photo on p. 94). With the plywood in place, it's time to measure the parts of the template and to trim, mark, and glue them all together.

Cut and prep the sink knockout

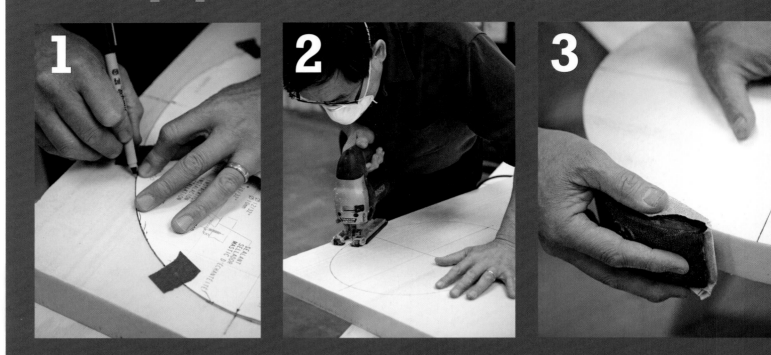

1 **Mark outline** Make sure the paper template will match your sink bowl. It should create a sink hole with the foam knockout that overhangs the sink by at least ¼ in. all around.

2 **Cut foam** Using a jigsaw fitted with a fine-tooth blade (or use a fine-tooth handsaw), cut the foam. If the foam is not the right thickness, cut as many pieces as you need to create the desired thickness.

3 **Sand edges** Smooth and square up the edges using a sanding block that's fitted with fine sandpaper.

4 **Mark centerline** After taking careful measurements, accurately mark the location of the sink on the foam knockout.

5 **Spray on adhesive** Cut a strip of clear Mylar® (or any flexible plastic sheet material cut to the thickness of your knockout) from a roll (see Resources on p. 102), and spray the strip with adhesive.

6 **Wrap with Mylar** After spraying on the adhesive, wrap the Mylar around the foam sink knockout to prevent concrete from sticking to it (you'll see how important this is later).

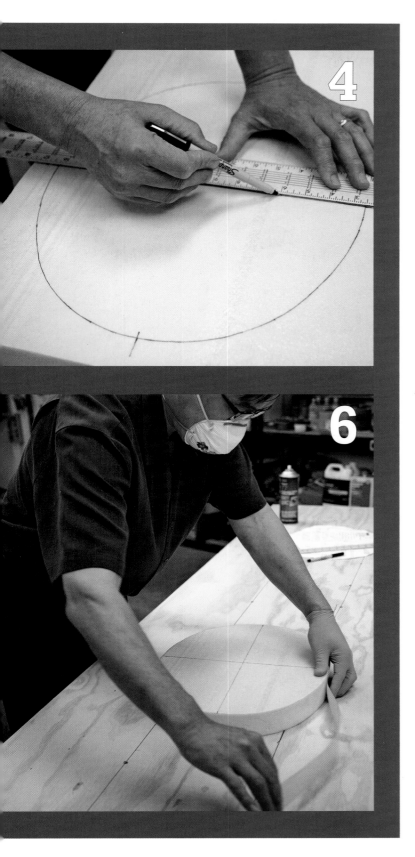

All about knockouts

Openings in the counter for the sink, faucets, sprayer, soap dispenser, and other accessories must be cast into the concrete as the counter is formed. There's no cutting them out later. Creating these openings is done using *knockouts,* which are blanks placed in the mold before the concrete is poured and then removed once the concrete has cured.

Making your own sink knockout

You can buy ready-made sink knockouts, which are available for popular sink sizes (see Resources on p. 102), or you can cut a custom knockout from pieces of rigid-foam insulation stacked to the full thickness of the counter. It's a little simpler if you use a sheet of foam that's just the right thickness, but built-up layers of foam work just as well. The sink you buy will come with a paper template showing the exact shape of the cutout. A concrete countertop always looks better overhanging the sink bowl by ¼ in. to ½ in., so check the paper template and see if it is the proper size. If it is too

Concrete at the edges

A sink can be undermounted directly to the countertop. Leave enough concrete "meat" around the knockouts to allow for mounting screws and anchors.

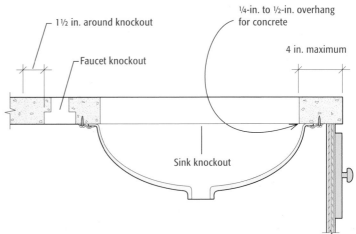

1½ in. around knockout

¼-in. to ½-in. overhang for concrete

Faucet knockout

4 in. maximum

Sink knockout

TEMPLATES THAT ADJOIN

If the template must be made in two or more pieces, don't overlap the adjoining sections. Instead, butt the sections end to end and make a mark or two to register the pieces so that they come together as planned.

Two-piece countertops

The template is a good indicator of when your countertop needs to be divided into two or more pieces. After all, if you have a hard time getting a 12-ft. template out of the room, imagine how hard it will be to handle a 12-ft., 1,000-lb. countertop. If access is through narrow hallways or around tight corners, a big countertop may not make it.

A 6-ft.-long countertop that's 2½ in. thick and 24 in. deep weighs approximately 400 lb. and takes four people to maneuver into place.

If you want to make a long countertop, limit the largest pieces to 8 ft. or less by 24 in. wide and 2½ in. thick. That's almost 4 cu. ft. of concrete, or 560 lb. If a counter is going to be longer, make it in sections that can be joined together.

This is done by inserting a thin divider, such as a piece of sheet metal or plastic, into the mold. You pour all the concrete at once. When the pieces are separated after demolding, the parts will line up and join perfectly. (See the top illustration below.)

However, if your work table is too short to make a single, long counter with a divider, then you must make sure that the two molds are perfectly matched at the joint so the pieces will line up later. (See the bottom illustration below.)

A countertop in two parts

If you need a longer countertop than we're showing in the book, you can cast one in two pieces. If space is at a premium, you can create a form in two separate pieces. To make the finished countertop easier and more manageable to move, you can cast it in two pieces together.

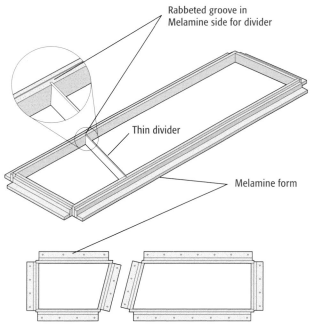

Rabbeted groove in Melamine side for divider

Thin divider

Melamine form

Two-piece countertop forms

large, shrink it down enough so that when you go to cut the foam sink knockout, it will be smaller than the sink bowl by at least ¼ in. (*Note:* If you are using a ready-made sink knockout, go straight to Step 5 on p. 28.)

Making faucet knockouts

Making the faucet knockouts is the simplest step involved in making the form, so I'm not going to complicate it by going into detail. You can buy ready-made rubber knockouts (see Resources on p. 102) or you can make your own from disks of plywood or foam.

Each faucet knockout will have two diameters, one atop the other: the small inside diameter for the stem of the faucet, typically 1⅜ in. in diameter, and a larger diameter that allows access for the faucet-mounting nut. That's usually 2⅞ in. in diameter. Wrap your homemade faucet knockouts with thin packing foam (⅛ in. thick) and packing tape. This will allow the knockout to "give" and release itself from the hardened concrete. Otherwise, you'll have a lot of trouble freeing the knockout from the countertop.

When you're finished, perform one last check to make sure your template is perfect, making sure it matches the location where it will be installed.

There's one last thing. Because the template will actually be used upside down to make the mold, remember to flip the template over and transfer all of the notations you've made from front to back.

Mark sink location

Precisely mark the sink location. To locate the holes for the faucets, you'll need to have the faucet on hand or know which model you plan to use. The number of holes needed depends on the type of faucet: A single-lever model, for example, needs a single hole, whereas a two-handle set requires a pair of holes placed at a specific distance apart.

Setting the faucet

The opening for the faucet, and therefore the knockout, requires two different diameters: one 1⅝ in. for the threaded faucet stem, and the other 2⅞ in. for the washer nut that will secure the faucet to the countertop. Structurally, it's also good to have at least 1¼ in. of concrete between the faucet opening and the sink opening.

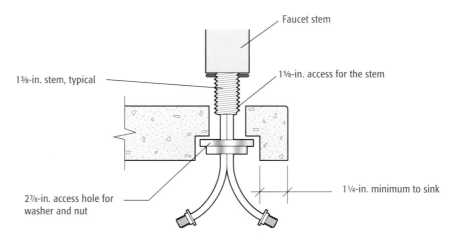

Faucet stem

1⅝-in. access for the stem

1⅜-in. stem, typical

2⅞-in. access hole for washer and nut

1¼-in. minimum to sink

Creating your own homemade pour table

Because concrete is so heavy (it weights about 150 pounds per cubic foot!), you'll need a good sturdy pour table to support the mold and its load of concrete and steel reinforcement. The table doesn't have to be a work of art—in fact, you can tear it apart for other uses when you're done. However, the two key requirements for the table are that it must be *strong* and it must be *level*. The table has to be able to support the concrete-filled mold without sagging, and it must be dead level so the concrete sets evenly. *Any* distortions (such as being thicker on one edge than on another) in the table and mold during the pour will become part of the finished countertop. Therefore buy dry, straight 2x4 lumber.

It has to be strong

Plan the pour table so it is at least 18 in. larger than the counter in both length and width. That will guarantee the mold is fully supported as the concrete cures and will give you a little breathing room. In our example, I'm building a pour table with some stout store-bought sawhorses, some 2×4s, and a 4x8 sheet of ¾-in. plywood. Remember, you won't be able to move the counter for several days after the pour, so put your pour table somewhere out of the way.

Once your pour table is built, you are ready to build the mold.

A sawhorse pour table

A sturdy pour table is essential for a flat countertop. You can build one over sawhorses with 2×4 stringers and a 4x8 ¾-in. plywood top that's screwed in place. The table should be shimmed so it's dead level. Space the 2×4s 9 in. to 10 in. apart.

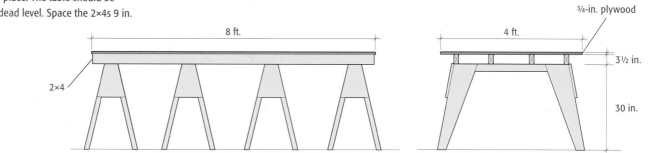

8 ft.

2×4

¾-in. plywood

4 ft.

3½ in.

30 in.

Make a sawhorse pour table

1 Space and fasten After lining up your sawhorses, place the 2×4s 9 in. to 10 in. apart across the sawhorses and fasten them in place with 2½-in. to 3-in. drywall screws.

2 Secure the plywood A 4x8 sheet of ¾-in. plywood is the right size. Simply level it on top of the assembly, and screw it securely to the 2×4s. Make sure the screws are flush with or slightly below the surface.

3 Shim and secure Finally, it is important to level up the sawhorses with shims. Use duct tape to fix the shims to the floor to avoid accidentally kicking them out of place and putting the table out of level. Use at least a 3-ft.-long level for an accurate read.

Making the mold

Building a mold is the next step and a critical one to the success of your countertop. With the template as a guide, we'll build a mold to the exact shape of the finished counter. It will include the sink and faucet knockouts as well as any inlay or detailing to jazz up the finished surface. For this counter, we're going to keep it simple and add a recess for a soap dish.

We assemble the mold on top of the pour table, which should be in an out-of-the-way spot that won't be disturbed while the concrete cures.

You can build your mold one of two ways. A newer technique is to use foam for the sides, a method I'll walk you through at the end of the chapter. The more common method is to use Melamine, the same ¾-in.-thick fiberboard sheet covered with durable plastic that we use for the bottom of the mold. It's flat, smooth, inexpensive, and available everywhere.

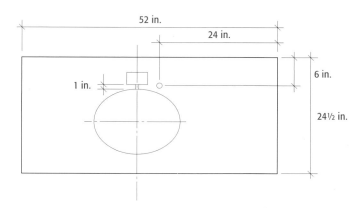

Cut sheet

Sides
(2) 52 in. × 2½ in. × ¾ in.
(2) 26 in. × 2½ in. × ¾ in.

Backer boards
(4) 50 in. × 2 in. × ¾ in.
(4) 22 in. × 2 in. × ¾ in.
(1) 1½-in. dowel
(1) 3-in. × 4½-in. × ⅜-in. soap knockout

Start with a drawing

In my shop, I start by making a schematic drawing of the counter based on the template. This plan should include all dimensions plus the exact locations for the faucet and sink knockouts. I can refer to this drawing whenever I need to get my bearings. Next, based on the drawing, I make a cut sheet, which is a list of all the parts, with all their dimensions, that I'll need to build the mold. One full sheet of Melamine will be enough to make the bottom and side walls for this counter.

For this part of the project a small, portable tablesaw is the most convenient tool for ripping sheet material, such as the Melamine and door skin. If you don't have a tablesaw and you can't rent one for a day, see if a local home center or cabinet shop can cut the pieces for you. Another option is to clamp down a straight length of wood on your work table as a guide, and use a circular saw to rip narrow strips of the Melamine. For fastening the pieces together, you'll need a drill/driver and countersinking bit.

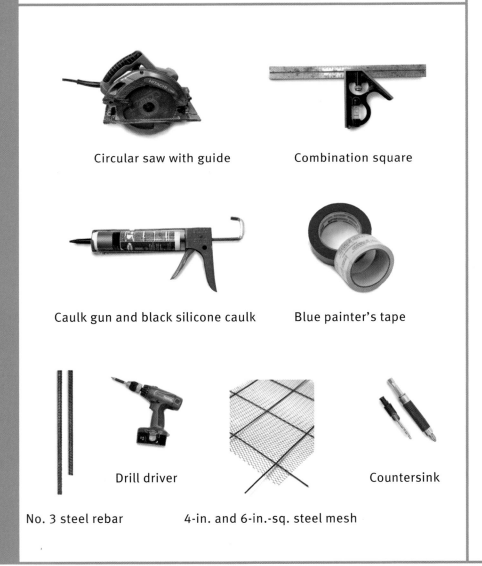

Circular saw with guide

Combination square

Caulk gun and black silicone caulk

Blue painter's tape

No. 3 steel rebar

Drill driver

4-in. and 6-in.-sq. steel mesh

Countersink

TOOLS AND MATERIALS

- Tablesaw or circular saw with guide for cutting the thin strips of Melamine for the sides of the form

- Hacksaw or right-angle grinder to cut the steel rebar that goes around the perimeter of the counter

- Combination square and Speed Square to spot check the mold's connections for right angles

- Drill/driver and countersinking bit for predrilling holes in the Melamine and for countersinking the screws

- Caulk gun and black silicone caulk for making all connections in the form

- A 4-ft. by 8-ft. sheet of Melamine, which will be cut into the necessary pieces to create the form

- Blue painter's tape for masking

- A supply of #8 by $1\frac{1}{2}$-in. and $1\frac{1}{4}$-in. drywall screws, to fasten the pieces of Melamine together

- No. 2 or 3 steel rebar for reinforcing

- Two short lengths of $\frac{1}{2}$-in. steel pipe for bending the rebar

- A roll of light gauge form wire

- 4-in.- and 6-in.-sq. steel mesh for additional reinforcing against cracking

The countertop is made upside down, so remember to flip the template over before building the mold.

A small portable tablesaw cuts the Melamine into strips for the form.

All the marks and notations you originally made on the template should be transferred to the back side.

Cutting and assembling

You will need narrow Melamine strips for the sides of the mold and backer braces that will hold the sides of the form in place when you pour in the concrete. With a tablesaw (or circular saw), cut the side pieces 3¼ in. wide (that's 2½ in. for the counter plus the ¾-in. thickness of the Melamine) and the backers 2 in. wide. Backers are formed in two pieces, making an L, so you'll need enough strips to go twice around the bottom. (For an alternate mold method, see "Consider making an instant foam mold" on p. 46.)

Because the countertop is made upside down, if you have not done so yet, you need to flip the template over before building the mold, so what was the top now faces down. All of the marks and notations you originally made

Classic mold

Melamine forms the sides and bottom in a classic countertop mold. Knockouts create voids in the concrete for the faucet and sink.

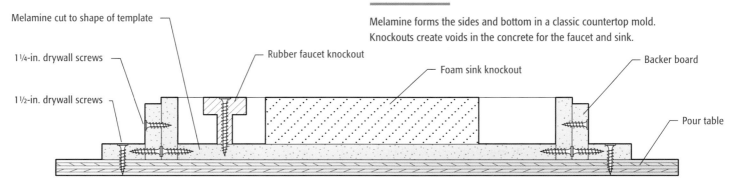

Melamine cut to shape of template

1¼-in. drywall screws

1½-in. drywall screws

Rubber faucet knockout

Foam sink knockout

Backer board

Pour table

on the template are transferred to the back side—the side that's now facing up. This is an easy thing to screw up—I know I've done it once or twice—so it's good to check and double-check everything.

Mark the outline of the template on the big Melamine base piece. I use blue painter's tape to hold the template in place while I work. Remember the finished counter will be an exact reproduction of the mold, so accuracy is essential if the finished counter is going to fit.

By the way, as you fasten the pieces of the mold together, spot check with your square to make sure everything is at right angles.

We'll use a circular saw with a guide clamped to the pour table to cut the Melamine to the exact template dimensions (following the lines transferred from your template). This will be the bottom of the mold assembly.

The sides of the form can be cut using a circular saw and guide.

Screw the pieces together

1 **Check for fit** After cutting the big Melamine base to the template outline (it was flipped over and all measurements and notes were transferred to the back of the template) bring your cut Melamine side pieces up to each side of the base and check for fit. Then mark sink center lines, faucets, and inlays on the Melamine base.

2 **Drill pilot holes** The side pieces are attached to the base with $1\frac{1}{2}$-in. drywall screws. To make it easier, draw a line along the side pieces $\frac{3}{4}$ in. back from one edge, then drill pilot holes midway between the edge and this line. Drill a hole every 6 in. to 8 in.

3 **Screw into base** Drive the screws through the pilot holes and into the edge of the base piece. Work your way around the bottom of the mold, and attach all of the side pieces. Be careful not to over-drill the screws.

4 **Fasten braces to sides** Now attach the L-shaped pieces to the sides of the mold. Before running the screws into the sides of the mold, remember to use the $1\frac{1}{2}$-in.-long screws because the tips of the longer screws could pop through the side of the mold. Supports are also screwed through the mold and into the top of the pour table.

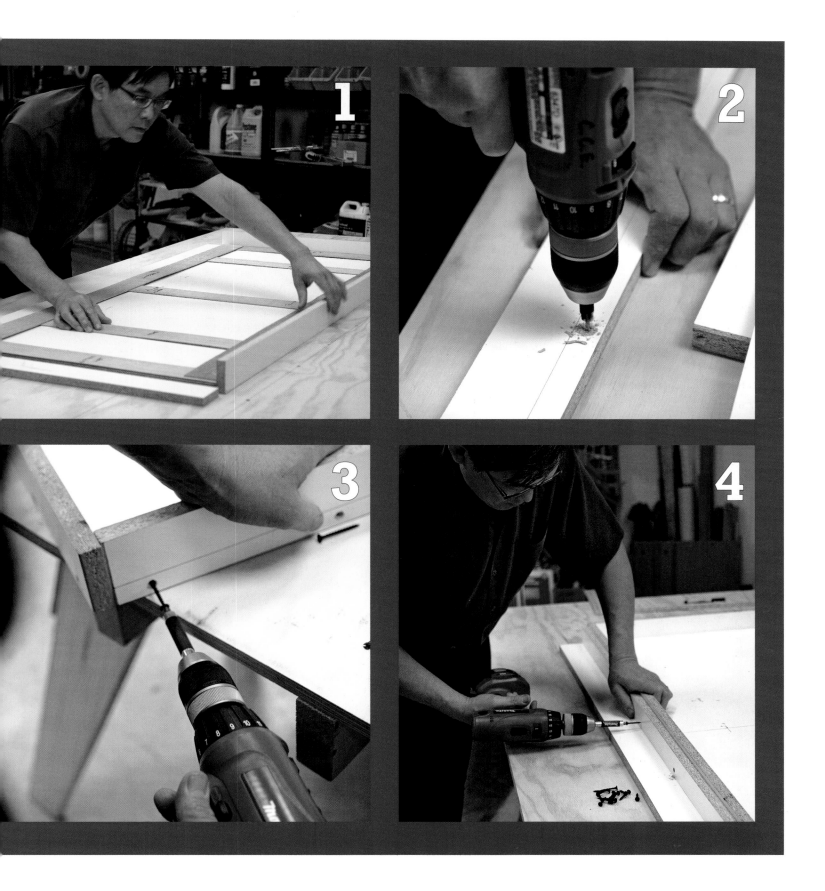

From the flipped-over template, transfer the rest of the information such as the centerline of the sink, the faucet holes, and the soap dish to the now-cut big Melamine base.

Putting the pieces together

You've now cut all the pieces of the mold and made sure the Melamine is clearly marked to represent the finished countertop. You should know which edge is which and where the sink and sink knockouts will be located in the mold.

Assembling the Melamine form

The form for the concrete countertop is made from smooth-finish Melamine and fastened together using drywall screws. In addition to the bottom (top) and sides, the plan calls for two brace strips for each side of the form, a total of 13 pieces of Melamine, all ripped and cut from one 4-ft. by 8-ft. sheet.

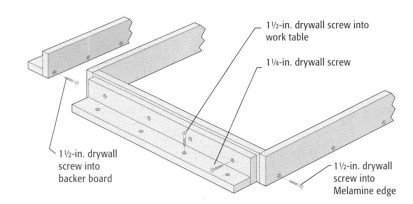

1½-in. drywall screw into work table

1¼-in. drywall screw

1½-in. drywall screw into backer board

1½-in. drywall screw into Melamine edge

Detailing accessories

1 Adhere the knockout When you're ready, run a bead of black silicone caulk on the backside of the sink knockout.

2 Press knockout in place After the back of the foam sink knockout is well caulked, position the knockout carefully on the layout marks, and press it firmly into place. Try not to smear the caulk out past the marks, but if you do, clean it up before moving forward.

3 Affix drain I'm adding a soap dish with a drain to this countertop. The drain channel that runs from the soap dish recess to the sink is formed from a short length of wood dowel cut in half lengthwise (the best way to do this is to carefully use a sharp utility knife). Unlike the sink and faucet knockouts, this won't go all the way through the countertop, so location in the mold is more aesthetic than critical. Here, I've centered it. Cover the outsides of the dowel with packing tape, and glue into place with caulk along the midline of the sink. Clean up the excess caulk with a cotton swab.

4 Add soap dish knockout The soap dish knockout is a thin piece of Masonite® hardboard, with slightly beveled edges, that's slightly larger than the wire soap dish I bought for the finished countertop. The beveled (sloped) edges keep the knockout from being trapped by the concrete when it cures, making it very difficult to remove. Just be sure to wrap the knockout in clear packing tape so it doesn't stick.

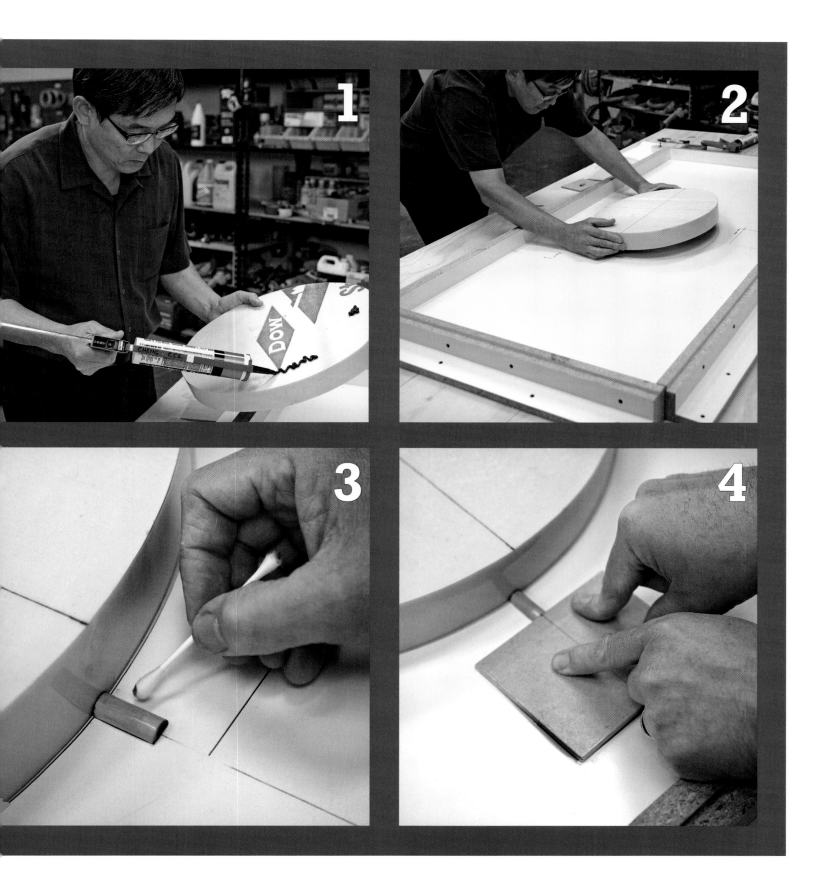

Tape, caulk, and peel

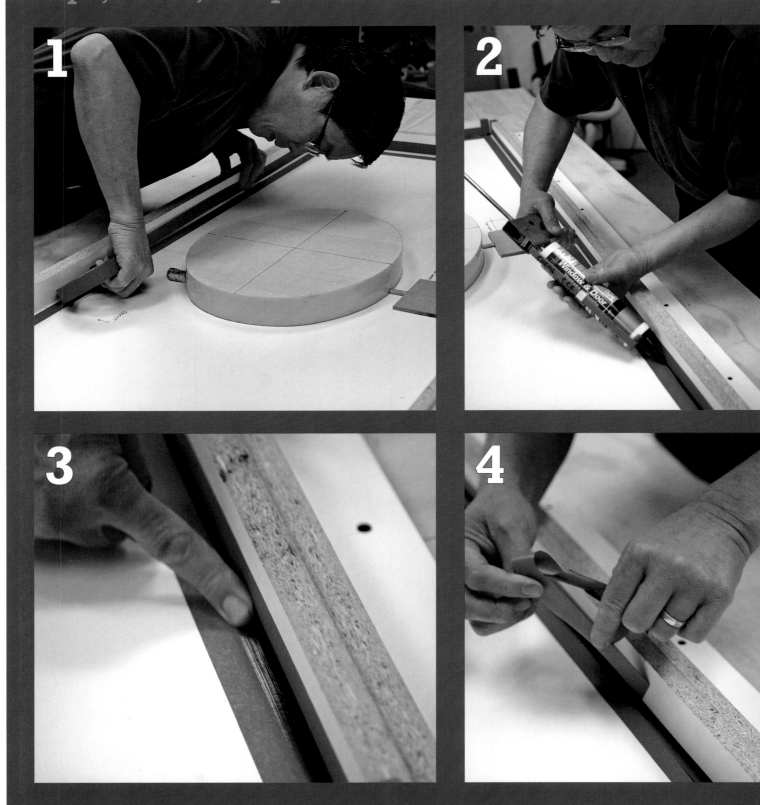

1 **Mask each joint** Using blue painter's tape, mask off all the joints to keep the caulk just where you want it. Keep the edge of the tape ⅛ in. back from both sides of the joint, and work your way all the way around the mold.

2 **Lay even caulk bead** Lay a ¼-in. bead of caulk evenly around the mold. Cutting the tip back to a 45-degree angle and angling the caulk gun will help you better control the flow of caulk. Try to work at a steady pace to keep the bead of caulk even. It's a good idea to practice your caulking application skills on a piece of scrap Melamine.

3 **Wet finger, smooth caulk** Now use a wetted finger to smooth the caulk. Go over it just once with your finger—don't keep trying to work the caulk into the joint. Work as smoothly as you can, but if there are minor imperfections, don't worry about them. *Note:* It's easy to mess this part up if you're not used to caulking, but if you do, don't try to rescue it by smoothing it again and again. The silicone will begin to skin over, and you will have a bigger mess. Leave the blue tape in place, remove all the silicone with a razor blade, wipe out the residue with a rag, and start over.

4 **Remove tape** Peel up the tape while the caulk is still wet, pulling the tape up and toward the joint as you go so you don't drag any of the caulk away from the seam. Let the silicone cure undisturbed for several hours.

Now we add the holes

The pieces are put together. The basic outlines of the mold are done. You can stand back now, look at it, and get a pretty good sense of its dimensions—height, width, depth. So it's time to start adding the knockouts and any little decorative details to the form (see pp. 40–41). You've already transferred the template marks to the Melamine bottom of the mold, so you know where the sink and faucet knockouts need to go.

Rounding and sealing the edges

The bottom inside edges of the mold will be the outside edges of the finished countertop. So think inside out for a minute: If you carefully caulk inside the corners of the mold and smooth them round, you will basically be rounding over the actual finished countertop edges—and that also makes them less likely to break off when we remove the mold. Also, concrete has a lot of water in it, which may cause problems with the mold if the particleboard core of the Melamine gets too wet. That is why all the seams around the mold, where edge pieces meet the bottom, should be sealed with 100-percent silicone caulk (not latex). I use black caulk because it's easier to see and, therefore, easier to clean up.

The first step in rounding out and sealing up the mold is to caulk all the joints where Melamine meets Melamine. Before caulking, apply blue painter's tape ⅛ in. back from the joints to keep the caulk just where you want it.

Sealing around the knockouts

After sealing all the Melamine joints, it's time to apply silicone around the sink, faucet, soap dish, and soap dish drain knockouts. The difference between this and caulking the Melamine joints is that it's fairly difficult to apply straight masking tape around circular objects, which means you're on your own—tapeless, as it were. So you need to summon all your steadiness at this point because, if you squeeze out too much silicone, there's no masking tape to catch the surplus goop.

Countertop-ready sticks of foam are available instead of Melamine to create the form for your pour. The foam mold is faster, easier, and requires fewer tools to construct but, of course, is not as strong as the Melamine.

Caulk the knockouts

1 Carefully caulk Steadily and carefully work your way around the knockout as you apply an even bead of silicon caulk.

2 Smooth bead Just like you did on the joints in the mold, use a wet finger to smooth the caulk around the perimeter of the knockout. Don't overwork the caulk.

3 Caulk the form-tape There may be a protruding lip of Mylar at the edge of the sink knockout that could cause problems when you place the concrete into the mold and smooth it out using a screed. So the last bit of caulking should fill any gaps between the edge of the Mylar and the foam of the knockout. After running a bead of caulk all the way around the knockout, smooth it out with a wet finger.

4 Place faucet knockout Now it's time for the faucet knockouts. Marks from the template should already be transferred to the bottom of the mold. Drill a small pilot hole at each knockout location, and set the tip of the knockout screw into the hole.

5 Screw knockout to base Use a drill/driver to fasten the knockout in place. Remember, the fat part of the knockout is on top and will form the recess for the nut that holds the faucet in place.

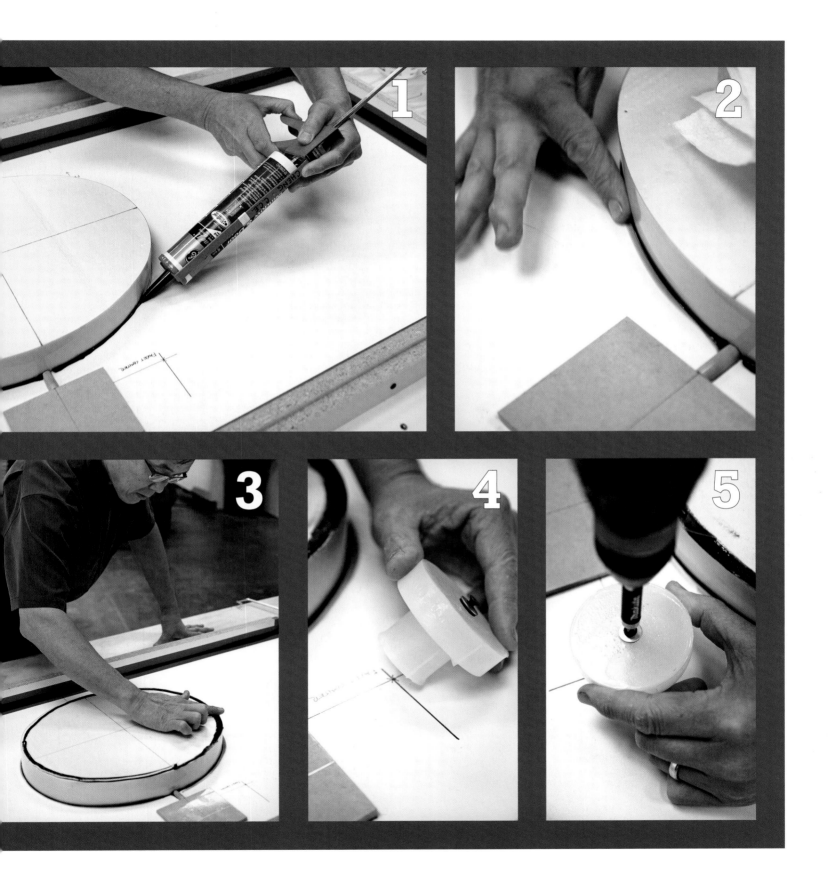

Consider making an instant foam mold

Now that you've seen how to build the traditional Melamine mold, here's a cool alternative method. With this new, convenient mold-making method you can have your mold ready to caulk and detail in less than 20 minutes. The foam works best with simple molds that don't have a lot of complex inlays along the edges.

No tablesaw needed

Precut foam sticks come in 2½-in.-thick, 6-ft. and 8-ft. lengths. The foam contains a special biodegradable resin and recycled foam content and uses a double-stick tape for strong adhesion.

You might want to experiment with this method using foam you buy locally. This is a great technique if you have limited access to power tools. However, you must be a bit more delicate handling and pouring concrete into these foam forms. The classic method of making backer boards and Melamine sides is still the best way to make tough and reusable molds, especially if they are complex.

Foam mold

Making a mold from pieces of foam is fast and easy, and the Melamine forming the bottom of the mold does not have to be cut to size. Adhesive-backed foam does not need backer boards for support.

Form a foam mold

1 Tape template to Melamine Place a 4-ft. by 8-ft. sheet of Melamine-coated sheet material on your pour table. Place your template on the sheet, but be sure to flip the template and transfer all relevant marks from the other side. Tape the template down in two places to prevent it from sliding.

2 Position tape Carefully apply the double-stick tape to the Melamine along the perimeter of the template, keeping it as close as possible to the template without it sticking to the template. Peel away the protective film when you're ready to place a foam side wall.

3 Apply foam securely Carefully place a piece of foam beside the template. Let it extend past the template at both ends, and don't let it stick to the exposed tape yet. Starting at one end, gradually and lightly adhere it to the tape, pushing the foam tight against the template. After applying foam to the opposite side, cut the other two sides to size and secure them.

4 Strengthen corners Push some finish nails into the corners, as shown, to add strength, and you are ready to caulk. Apply Mylar liner tape, or any flexible plastic, to the inside of the foam if it doesn't already have it, and place some inexpensive right-angle brackets against the foam to support wire reinforcing. Now you are ready to caulk.

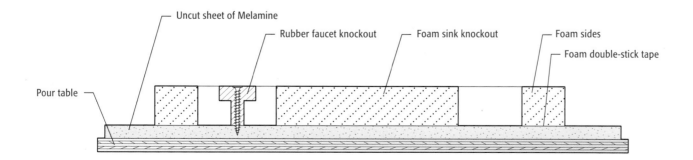

Uncut sheet of Melamine
Rubber faucet knockout
Foam sink knockout
Foam sides
Foam double-stick tape
Pour table

Making your countertop even stronger

Despite concrete's great compressive strength, it can still use some help when it comes to resisting bending loads, like those you would expect to get on a countertop. Also, some parts of the counter are relatively thin, like the area around the sink. To help keep this countertop strong, we'll insert two kinds of steel reinforcement: ¼-in. or ⅜-in. rebar and a layer of 4-in. by 4-in. steel mesh.

For basic countertops under 6 ft. long that don't have long sinks, rebar isn't an absolute necessity and simple steel mesh will do. However, rebar adds extra strength to any countertop. And if you want a large, undermount sink you'll need the rebar to help reinforce the narrow span of concrete running along the length of the sink.

Another way to make the concrete stronger is to add fibers to the concrete mix, which will make the countertop less likely to develop little cracks. A variety

Reinforcing the concrete

A combination of 4-in. welded wire mesh and ⅜-in. rebar suspended near the middle of the mold helps make the countertop stronger and less susceptible to cracking.

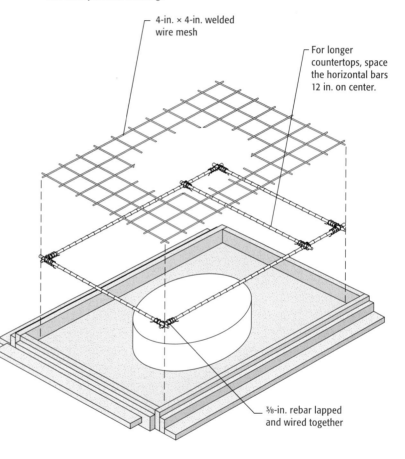

4-in. × 4-in. welded wire mesh

For longer countertops, space the horizontal bars 12 in. on center.

⅜-in. rebar lapped and wired together

Making it stronger

As strong as it is, concrete needs reinforcement. Unreinforced concrete can crack under a bending load. When the load is in the middle of the concrete, embed the rebar below the centerline. For a cantilevered counter, locate the rebar above the centerline.

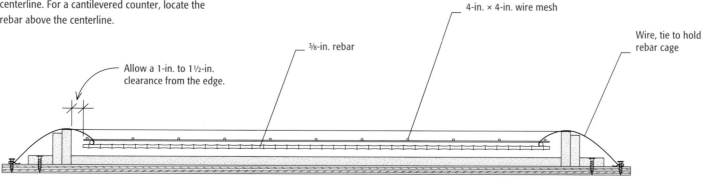

Allow a 1-in. to 1½-in. clearance from the edge.

⅜-in. rebar

4-in. × 4-in. wire mesh

Wire, tie to hold rebar cage

DOUBLE-CHECK YOUR WORK

Once the concrete is added to the form, we use a straightedge (called a screed) to flatten the concrete and level it out with the form. To ensure that the concrete countertop will be flat and even the top edges of the mold are used as a guide for running the leveling screed, which is simply a long, straight piece of the Melamine used in a sawing motion from one side to the other to level and flatten from front and back.

So before you pour the concrete use a straightedge to check to make sure the screed will pass smoothly over the knockouts for the sink and faucets. Now is the time to make minor adjustments. It's better to shave a bit here and there than to get caught with a mold full of hardening concrete.

Before proceeding with forming and installing the steel reinforcement, double-check all your measurements to avoid headaches later. Also use a straightedge to ensure that the knockout heights are right.

of fibers are on the market. Most countertop admixtures, like the Pro-Formula I use, have just the right proportion of very fine nylon fibers to prevent undue cracking. And these fibers won't show on the finished surface. Use caution if you decide to add your own to a mix: Most fibers are designed for use in large slabs that have a rough surface when finished so unsightly fibers aren't an issue.

Let's add some steel

A steel-reinforced countertop is stronger and less likely to crack than an unreinforced one. For some large, complicated concrete countertops, a complex grid of rebar is required around and throughout the concrete. For this counter, it's enough to form the rebar into a simple rectangle to go around the outside of the mold. Just remember to keep the rebar at least 1½ in. from the counter's edge and from the sink knockout and 1½ in. from the bottom of the concrete or, in other words, slightly closer to the top of the mold than to the bottom.

Before adding the reinforcing steel (rebar and steel mesh) to the form, vacuum the form thoroughly to remove debris, wood chips, and anything else that could become part of the counter and mar the finished top. This is also the time to make sure the heights of the sink and faucet knockouts are correct by running a rigid straightedge across the mold.

Now let's bend a piece of rebar to go around the perimeter of the counter. You can borrow or rent a bender made specifically for rebar or use a vise and a length of pipe to slip over the rebar as a cheater. Cut the steel using a hacksaw or right-angle grinder (wear safety glasses).

Bend the rebar into shape by holding it in a vise and slipping an iron pipe over one end for leverage. Once the rebar is bent to shape, rest it in the mold temporarily on pieces of 1-in.-thick foam. Once it's fitted, lift it out and again vacuum the bottom of the mold before placing the steel cage back into the mold.

Bend and place the steel

1 Cut mesh to fit Cut the steel mesh so it fits around the sink knockout. Just keep the wire far enough away from the sides of the mold and the sink knockout so it won't show up in the finished counter.

2 Connect rebar to mesh Make the rebar cage and the wire mesh one piece by tying the two together using form wire.

3 Wire rebar in place To keep the wire assembly at the correct height in the mold, suspend it with form wire (light wire used to tie rebar, available at hardware stores). The wire goes up over the top edge of the mold and is wrapped around screws set into the top of the pour table.

THE ART OF INLAYS

Inlays are hard, flat objects that you want to show up on the surface of your countertop. Inlays can be an expression of art, whimsy, or personal fancy. Shells, fossils, coins, jewelry, rubber stamps—each can be used to add a touch of personal detail to your countertop.

Inlays are fixed to the mold using silicone, which is strong enough to hold the inlay during vibration of the wet concrete yet forgiving enough to release the insert when removing the countertop from the mold.

To fix to the mold, spread a paper-thin layer of silicone caulk on each inlay using a razor blade and press it into the bottom of the mold. Be careful not to apply a thick layer of silicone, because the inlay will be depressed instead of flush with the finished concrete surface.

Decorative aggregates (semiprecious stones such as turquoise, mother-of-pearl, and amazonite) are an additional way to personalize your countertop. Most decorative aggregates are ¼ in. or smaller and usually are not flat on one side. To apply silicone to each one would be tedious. The best way to hold them to the mold surface is to lightly mist the mold with a coating of spray adhesive then quickly sprinkle the decorative aggregates while the adhesive is still tacky. Figure that at least half of the stones will get lost while you're vibrating the mix, so use more aggregate than you think you will need.

Stone inlays   Machine part inlays   Tile inlays

Mixing and pouring

The mold is ready, and now it's time to wade right in and get your hands dirty. This part of the process is exciting because the preliminaries are over, and you'll finally get to see the countertop take shape.

Just like making a template and then building a mold, mixing and placing the concrete calls for working carefully and methodically. But time itself is now a factor. Because mixed concrete can sit around for only so long, get all of the tools and materials you'll need and round up at least one other person to give you a hand.

A bag of premixed concrete contains cement powder, sand, and graded aggregate (rocks). Just be sure to wear a dust mask to avoid breathing in the fine dust.

Understanding the basic mix

In the past, if you made concrete countertops for a living, you would probably mix your own concrete from scratch. You'd gather cement, fine and coarse aggregate, graded sand, and water—and mix them all in the right proportions. However, as somebody who has done this professionally for years, I can promise you that it's a lot easier to go to your local home center or hardware store and buy bagged concrete mix. At least some of the time-consuming work has already been done for you. It's all been premeasured and weighed out for you in convenient bags.

Now we get to the heavy part. For the mix you'll need concrete, water, admixture, and heavy-duty tools to get the job done right.

Bag of concrete mix

Clean water and hose with nozzle

Cement mixer

Wheelbarrow

Concrete trowel

Rubber gloves

Vibrating tool

Admixture

Pails

TOOLS AND MATERIALS

- A hose with a nozzle for controlling the flow of water

- An electric or gas-powered cement mixer is preferable but you can mix in a wheelbarrow

- A concrete vibrating tool to keep air pockets to a minimum, which creates a smooth, blemish-free countertop surface

- Wheelbarrow

- A shovel for moving the wet mix in small batches

- Wire cutters

- Concrete trowel for placing and smoothing the wet mix

- One or two 5-gal. pails for rinsing and washing

- Safety equipment: dust mask, heavy-duty rubber gloves, hearing protection

- Shop apron to protect your clothes

- 3 cu. ft. (six 60-lb. bags) 5,000 psi concrete mix

- A ready source of clean water for mixing the concrete

- Admixture containing pigments for color, fibers for strength, and other conditioners that make concrete workable (if you plan on making your own, see "Make it from scratch" on p. 56)

- A scrap of Melamine 18 in. longer than the width of the form to use as a screed

- A quantity of plastic sheeting to cover the mixer, mask off dry areas, and tent the final pour

On top of the dry concrete mix, you add the proper amount of pigment and dry admixtures. These need to be thoroughly mixed in the cement mixer before the water is added.

I recommend you buy high-strength 5,000 pounds per square inch (psi) bagged concrete (make sure it's not the "air-entrained" variety). If that's unavailable, you can do one of two things: buy ordinary bagged concrete, which is rated at 2,500 psi, and add 3 lb. to 4 lb. of pure cement powder to every 60-lb. bag or mix your own formula from scratch (see "Make it from scratch" on p. 56).

Admixtures

The countertop we're building contains 3 cu. ft. of concrete, which means you'll need four to six bags of 5,000-psi concrete. They come in two sizes: ½-cu.-ft., 60-lb. sacks and ⅔-cu.-ft., 80-lb. sacks. Always buy a little more concrete than you think you'll need. You don't want to run short.

Once you have your basic 5,000-psi concrete, using a prepared professional countertop-grade admixture with all of the right ingredients in the right proportions saves a lot of time and trouble. Everything you need is already in it. There are several brands on the market (see Resources on p. 102). But if you decide to make your own admixture, gather up the ingredients you'll need (see p. 56).

For a good batch of concrete, all the ingredients must be mixed thoroughly. This is where a cement mixer is a big help. It not only takes the drudgery out of the process but allows you to make the concrete in larger batches. A 12-cu.-ft. mixer is ideal for this 3-cu.-ft. project. Just so you know, in practical terms, a 12-cu.-ft. mixer will handle only 6 cu. ft. of concrete; a 6-cu.-ft. mixer will handle only 3 cu. ft. of concrete.

Let's start by mixing all of the dry ingredients thoroughly. Once you've got all of your tools and ingredients assembled, including water and a hose with a nozzle, don your dust mask and gloves, open the bags of concrete mix, and pour them into the mixer.

Make it from scratch

If you decide to make your own base mix, these proportions are calculated per cubic foot:

- Type II or type III cement, 23 lb.
- $^3/_8$-in. pea gravel, 37 lb.
- Graded sand, 72 lb.
- Water, 7 lb. to 9 lb.

To make you own admixture to add to the premixed concrete, the following are the minimum additional ingredients you'll need to approximate commercial admixtures.

PIGMENT Pigment is usually iron oxide–based mineral colors in powder or liquid form. Do not add more than 6 lb. of any color to this 3-cu.-ft. batch of concrete. (Approximately 10 percent of the cement powder in 3 cu. ft.)

NYLON FIBERS Fibers reduce the amount of potential hairline cracks that may form; 1 oz. or 2 oz. will be plenty.

PLASTICIZER Also called water reducer, plasticizer allows the concrete to flow into the form without your needing to add too much water. For 3 cu. ft., you will need less than 1 qt. Generally, this is available commercially only in 20-gal. (or larger) containers. It's available on-line in smaller quantities.

Mix the concrete

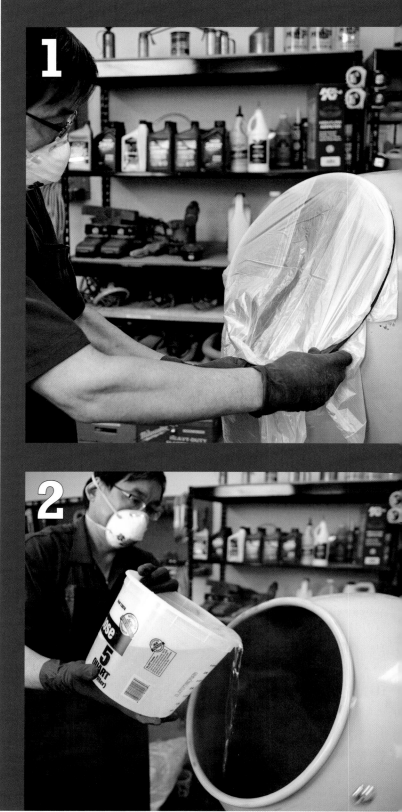

1 Cover and mix Open the admixture and check to make sure the ingredients haven't clumped up. If so, knead and break up the clumps with your gloved hands. Add the admixture to the dry mixture and mix the dry ingredients thoroughly. To keep the dust level down, cover the mouth of the mixer with a piece of plastic. Use Bungee® cords to hold the plastic in place; run the mixer for a couple of minutes, and then check to see that the admixture is evenly distributed.

2 Add water and run mixer Next, add the amount of water recommended on the bag of admixture or concrete mix, and let the mixer run for several minutes.

3 Resist adding more water The mix may first appear lumpy and dry, but don't be tempted to add lots of water right away. Follow the specific instructions for water content that comes with your prepared admixture. Soupy concrete is weak and will crack and shrink as it cures.

4 Test mix After the mixer has run for several minutes, stop the mixer, don a glove, and grab a gob to check how the concrete is doing.

5 Rest, mix, and retest Let the batch rest for 2 minutes, and then continue running the mixer. If you have to add any more water put in just a little at a time. The whole mix process will take between 10 minutes and 15 minutes. When mixed, the concrete should be the consistency of runny oatmeal. With the professional admixture I am using the water reducer allows the mix consistency to be runnier without compromising strength. Add enough water to make the mix workable.

Make the pour

1 Scoop, pour, and push Scoop up some concrete from the wheelbarrow with your 5-gal. bucket and pour it into the mold, working your way around the form. Use your gloved hands to push and work the concrete into the steel reinforcement and around the knockouts. Don't bump anything out of place. Fill the form half to two thirds full.

2 Force out air Make sure there are no voids in the concrete, and try to work out any trapped air, first with you're your gloved hands, then with the vibrator.

3 Vibrate below surface While a helper continues placing concrete, work the vibrator back and forth just beneath the surface for several minutes to drive out air pockets that may be on the bottom of the mold (the top of the counter). Be careful; if the tool comes into contact with an inlay, it could move it out of place. If the vibrator splatters concrete all over the place, put plastic sheeting over your work zone and slide the tool beneath the plastic.

4 Top off and jiggle Now top off the mold with concrete to slightly over full. You can jiggle the pour table to help settle the concrete. Don't try to work the concrete too hard, but use firm and friendly shaking to consolidate the mix.

To get the wet concrete mix to the form, dump a load of it into a wheelbarrow and truck it to the table. Let the concrete rest a while before pouring it into the form.

It starts to take shape

Now is the time to check if the mix "feels" right. Add water to get the mix workable, which means it can readily flow into the nooks and crannies of your mold when you're using the vibrator (check the manufacturer recommendation). You now need to transfer the mixed concrete into a good, sturdy wheelbarrow—something that can handle some weight—and get it over to the pour table. Before you pour, allow the concrete to rest for about 10 minutes. Then remix the concrete in the wheelbarrow with a shovel or hoe before you scoop it up and start pouring.

Screed and trowel

1 Use sawing motion Using a 2x4 as a screed and starting on your left at one end of the concrete-filled mold, slowly saw the 2x4 back and forth from front to back, all the while moving to your right. Apply a steady downward pressure as you work.

2 Gather excess concrete As you work the 2x4 across the mold, you will gather a rising wave of extra concrete. Keep pushing it along as you saw the screed from front to back.

3 Screed off excess Continue screeding, but take care not to damage the foam sink knockout. Now you can push the excess concrete off onto the table, where you can scrape it off into a bucket.

4 Begin troweling With most of the excess concrete removed from your mold, begin gliding your steel concrete trowel across the surface of the concrete. Resist working the concrete too aggressively.

5 Even up surface Exerting a slight pressure on the back side of the trowel—away from the lightly raised forward edge—continue to stroke the trowel evenly across the concrete until you have cleared away all the excess concrete and leveled the surface.

Screeding and smoothing the wet concrete

Now we do what we can while the concrete is still wet and pliable to make sure that the cured concrete countertop is as smooth as possible. Although we're only smoothing the bottom of the countertop, we want it smooth and even so, once we install it, the countertop sits level. To get this even smoothness requires screeding and troweling.

The process requires a little elbow grease and some haste. To get started, grab a scrap of leftover Melamine or a 2x4 as a screed—a kind of a big scraper. The purpose of screeding is to remove excess concrete from the mold; this is followed by troweling the concrete to a flat surface.

If you are using the foam mold technique, the sides of the mold are quite fragile, so you must be extremely careful to screed the excess concrete off gently.

Vibrating

Before leaving the concrete to cure, snip off the form wire that is holding up the rebar, and tuck the ends into the concrete.

Vibration is the best way to reduce the air pockets in the surface of your countertop. Use a professional concrete vibrator, which you should be able to find at most tool rental shops. Rent the smallest size possible, which is usually a model with a head diameter of 1 in. or less.

It's better to vibrate the concrete in layers, not all at once. After partially filling the mold, work the head of the vibrator around the rebar, taking care not to knock anything out of place. The procedure should take about 5 minutes. Once you've topped off the mold with concrete, vibrate for a final time. Vibrate against the sides and bottom of the mold. (This process is not for foam molds.)

Drape a piece of plastic over the entire countertop after it has been smoothed with the finishing trowel. Keep it there for up to four days to allow the concrete to "cure" (hydrate) slowly.

Tying up loose ends

Before you leave the concrete to cure, you still have a few more simple tasks to do.

When the concrete has firmed up a bit, take a pair of wire cutters and snip off the form wire that's holding up the rebar inside the concrete and tuck the ends of the wire beneath the surface.

Curing

Now you need to cover the concrete with a damp blanket or a sheet of plastic. The counter needs to cure in a warm, humid environment for 4 days. Do not cure the countertop in the sun because it can dry out too fast and develop cracks. The temperature should be between 60° and 90°F (75° is ideal) with a humidity greater than 25 percent.

If you are working in a chilly garage or shop, you can fashion a tent over the form with plastic sheeting and place a small baseboard-type radiant heater under the pour table. Make sure you don't create a fire hazard (avoid electric-coil, kerosene, and propane heaters), and don't cook the concrete.

In very hot and dry conditions, you can cover the form with very moist old carpet and then tent it. That reduces moisture loss and allows a slow, moist cure.

After 4 days to 6 days (if your conditions are ideal) you should notice the counter pulling away ever so slightly from the mold. That's a sign that the counter is ready to be released from the mold. If the temperatures have been in the low range (55° to 65°F), allow a few more days of curing time. If the temperature has been in the high range, keep a wet carpet over the piece and a plastic tent over the carpet to retain moisture.

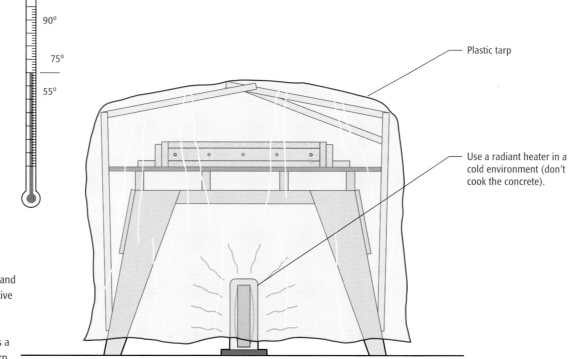

Plastic tarp

Use a radiant heater in a cold environment (don't cook the concrete).

Curing tent

Concrete cures best in temperatures between 55° and 90°F (75° is ideal) and relative humidity greater than 25 percent. A radiant heater beneath the pour table plus a tent made from a plastic tarp can help tame adverse conditions.

Out of the mold

After curing for 4 days, the concrete is still "green," meaning it hasn't reached complete hardness. At this point it is hard enough to be popped out of the mold but still soft enough to be vulnerable to scratching. This is a job that requires some finesse because the counter will crack if it's flexed or twisted. To make sure the release goes smoothly, round up a couple of friends to help—in fact, it wouldn't hurt to get three friends. Later, you can return the favor when they're making their own concrete countertop.

Removing the sides of the mold

Just as you put the mold together in a certain order back in Step 2, so you take it apart. We start by removing the L-shaped Melamine braces that buttress the sides of the mold. Then we remove all of the screws that hold the mold together. Just double-check to make sure you've gotten every single screw.

Use gentle persuasion

"Try a Little Tenderness" could be this chapter's theme song. Protecting the concrete surface and edges while removing the form requires a soft touch.

The first step in removing your countertop from the form is to unscrew the L-shaped braces reinforcing the sides of the mold.

L ike a surgeon preparing for an operation, you'll need a selection of specific tools on hand before you start taking the concrete out of the mold.

TOOLS AND MATERIALS

- A good finish hammer for delivering gentle blows to the prybar or shim

- Drill/driver with a no. 2 Phillips® bit

- Blocks of 1-in.-thick rigid-foam insulation to cushion the countertop when you flip it over

- Prybar to ease between the pieces of the Melamine form

- Single-edge razor or utility knife to scrape off excess caulk or concrete from the knockouts as you remove them

- A file for easing the sharp edges of the concrete after the form is removed

- Wooden shims to gently pry apart pieces of Melamine

- Flathead screwdrivers for gently prying the bottom off the form

- An awl for help in removing the knockouts

- Plastic or tarp for water protection

- Sponges

Hammer

Drill/driver with a no. 2 Phillips bit

Steel file

Awl

Utility knife

After removing the screw that holds the faucet knockout to the Melamine base, carefully work a couple of flat-head screwdrivers into the knockout material; avoid prying directly against the concrete.

Removing faucet knockouts

With the side pieces removed, back out the screw that holds the faucet knockout in place before trying to pry out the knockout. You can use two flat-head screwdrivers to work it free, but try not to pry against the concrete itself. Work the screwdriver tips in against the upper edge of the knockout and work it out carefully. You also will want to ease the edges of the concrete by rounding over the length of the edges with a file.

Dulling sharp edges

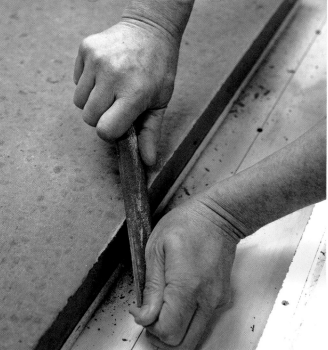

Dulling sharp edges

You'll notice that the edge of the concrete is sharp when the side pieces of the mold are removed. Before going any further we want to ease these edges. If something were to catch the edge of the counter as it was being flipped over, it could chip away part of the concrete and make a divot that you'd see when the counter is installed. Gently rounding over the edges will head off that potential problem. You can use a diamond pad, a masonry stone, or a file. Work your way around the counter and ease the edges using gentle, even pressure on the tool.

Remove the sides

1 Pry with care Start at one corner by gently working a small prybar between the ends of two side pieces. Remember, the concrete is still somewhat delicate, so keep the prybar away from the concrete, and push and pry gently against the Melamine.

2 Open a gap Pry the side piece away, making a gap big enough to get your fingers between the Melamine and the concrete.

3 Slowly peel apart Then grasp the end of the side piece and pull slowly with constant pressure to spring the Melamine away from the concrete.

4 Pry only against Melamine To remove the two end pieces, tap the top edge of the Melamine with a hammer. This should be enough to knock them loose. If not, work a wooden shim gently between each side piece and the bottom of the mold and tap gently with a hammer until the gap is big enough for your fingers. You can also use a screwdriver to open a gap by placing the tip between the end piece and bottom Melamine of the mold and tapping gently. Keep the screwdriver away from the concrete itself.

Be sure to use foam scraps to cushion the edge of the fresh-formed concrete before turning over the counter.

Turning the mold over

To remove the bottom of the mold, the counter has to be turned over. If it is 3 ft. or 4 ft. long, you'll need at least one extra helper, but if it's at all longer, you must enlist the help of three of your beefy friends and neighbors. The countertop/Melamine assembly has to be lifted to a vertical position, then gently allowed to land on its opposite side. This is a tricky move (and a potentially dangerous one), and the counter can suddenly shift or drop. Make sure everyone knows his or her position, is vigilant, and is sober—save any six-pack payoffs until *after* the job is over. Everyone should be wearing gloves to protect fingers.

The Melamine can be stubborn in coming off so at this stage a bit of patience is in order. If you're not careful you can scar the countertop, so take special care to prevent damage. Remember, the concrete is still not yet fully cured.

All that should be left of the original form are the knockouts for the sink, the soap dish and its drain, and the little decorative recess on the front edge of the countertop that we created to hold a small piece of decorative turquoise.

Now leave it alone

The concrete should be allowed to cure for an additional 2 days to 3 days before you begin the next step, which is polishing the surface.

Each day of curing makes for harder concrete. Don't rush this. Wait any less than 2 full days, and the concrete may be too soft to polish—it will tear because not all of the aggregate will be firmly embedded and you'll end up with a rough surface. Keep the counter in the same warm, humid environment as you did for the initial curing process.

Again, do not cure it in direct sunlight.

3

1 Position foam cushioning Slide the counter to one long edge of the pour table so that a little less than half of it hangs over the edge. Space pieces of 1-in.-thick rigid-foam insulation (or something similar) underneath and along the long edge of the Melamine that sits on the pour table and place some on the opposite side of the table, where the countertop will land.

2 Rest concrete on foam Now carefully lift the entire assembly so the counter/Melamine assembly is resting vertically on its edge *on pieces of foam*. The foam serves two purposes: It cushions the countertop in case of a sudden release, and it prevents your fingers from being crushed.

Caution: The concrete can suddenly release itself from the Melamine and slip to one side or even off the table if you're not careful; be vigilant!

3 Lower concrete carefully After making sure the foam blocks are in place, lower the counter carefully down to the pour table. Easy does it. Be careful to hold the concrete and not the Melamine as you handle the counter since the mold could release under pressure. And try not to flex, twist, or bend the counter, which can cause small cracks in the concrete.

Extract knockouts

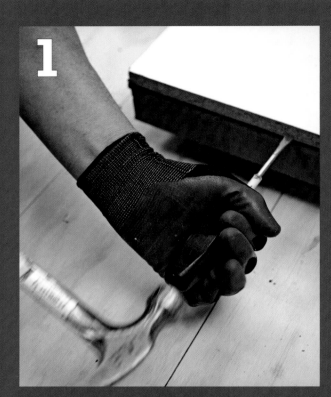

1 Drive it in Drive the tip of a flat-head screwdriver carefully into the Melamine itself, making sure you drive it in deep and that it is as secure as possible.

2 Drive in second handle Now drive a second flat-head screwdriver into the Melamine toward the other end of the base. What you're trying to do is to make two handles to lift the Melamine off the countertop without touching the concrete at all.

3 Grasp and pull slowly Once you can grasp the Melamine, pull upward slowly and steadily to release the bottom of the mold from the concrete. It should pop off without too much trouble.

4 **Pry out dish and drain** Pop out the knockouts for the soap dish and the drainage channel. The sharp tip of an awl is a good tool here. Take care not to pry against the concrete as you work the knockouts free. Any inlays in the concrete will have a thin layer of silicone caulk on them. Use a single-edge razor to scrape away any excess caulk or concrete that covers them.

5 **Remove decorative knockout** On the front 2½-in. face of this counter, I used a small furniture bumper (available at a hardware store) to create a recess to frame a piece of polished stone. Prick this out with the awl. This will make room for a nice detail on the front face of the finished countertop.

6 **Knock out sink knockout** Now the sink knockout can be removed. This may be easier to do with the counter up on edge (cushioned with the foam). Get your helpers (I hope you haven't yet opened any of those six-packs) to hold the counter firmly while you remove the knockout and the piece of Mylar that separated it from the concrete. This is a good time to practice that kung fu punch.

Polish
and slurry

**O**ur countertop is out of the mold but not quite finished. Giving it a good polish is the next step. Polishing does more than make it shine, it's a great way of eliminating blemishes on the surface and exposing the beauty of the natural aggregates. The abrasive tools we'll use range from hand diamond pads to diamond disks mounted on a variable-speed polisher.

Making it shine

Diamond disks work on concrete just like sandpaper works on wood. The only difference is that, with diamonds on concrete, the surface needs to be lubricated with water, which also keeps things cool and holds down dust. Of course, electricity and water don't mix, so there are several very important safety precautions you must take before getting started (see "Play It Safe" on p. 77).

Like sandpaper, each diamond disk is numbered. The lower the number, the coarser the grit. The higher the number, the finer the grit and the higher the polish you'll get. The disks we'll use range from 50 grit all the way up to 1,500 grit.

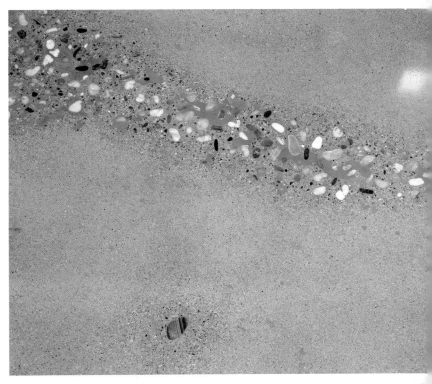
Polishing reveals the fine sand and scattered decorative aggregate just beneath the surface.

After using 50-grit and 100-grit sanding disks to expose as much aggregate as you want, begin using finer grits.

Like every other step of the way in our countertop-making process, there are certain tools and materials you'll need. Here's a list of what you'll want on hand for polishing.

- Variable-speed polisher, under 3,000 rpm, preferably with a water feed or an orbital sander as a substitute

- Rubber gloves to protect your hands from the abrasives

- Ground-fault circuit interrupter (GFCI), connected to a verifiable grounded outlet, to prevent electric shock

- Rubber squeegee to squeeze water and grit off the concrete surface

- Plastic putty knife for spreading the slurry mix

- Container for mixing the slurry compound, a soupy mixture of water and cement dust

- Measuring cup for slurry ingredients

- A rubber apron to protect your clothes

- Spray bottle for keeping the countertop wet

- Diamond disks, used wet, for polishing the surface to a high shine

- Wet/dry diamond hand pads for hard-to-reach areas

- Ample and constant water supply

- Lots of rags for cleaning up and wiping down

- Slurry mix for filling any tiny holes that appear during polishing

Diamond disks

Rubber gloves

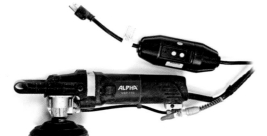

Variable-speed polisher
(1,200 to 3,000 rpm)

Wet/dry diamond
hand pads

Plastic putty knives

Rubber squeegee

Working with a messy, wet surface

This part of the process is messy so place some 2x4s on edge on the perimeter of your pour table. Then cover them with a plastic tarp to form a reservoir for the water-polishing process.

To start, run water over the countertop to give it a thorough cleaning. You'll need a constant supply of water on the surface as you polish, which makes a polisher with a central water feed the best tool for the job (you can rent these or get your own for about $300). If you don't have one or can't rent one, you can—as we show—use a random-orbit sander. Instead of a constant water feed, get a small plastic container that has few holes drilled in it near the bottom so water seeps out and keeps the surface of the concrete wet. Or keep a big sponge in plastic bucket full of water nearby and squeeze water on the concrete as needed. Be sure to double-check for frayed cords, and make sure your orbital sander is double insulated. *It will take twice the time to polish with the sander than with a proper polisher.*

Pick the right disk

The disk you choose for the initial polish depends on how much of the aggregate in the concrete you want to expose. If you want to show a lot of aggregate, start with a 50-grit disk. If you don't want much aggregate to be exposed in the finished surface, start with a 400-grit disk.

Get to polishing

Plug the polisher or sander into a ground-fault circuit interrupter (GFCI), which in turn should be plugged into a grounded, three-prong outlet; then go ahead and get started. Here I'm using a random orbit sander and a sponge with a bucket of water at hand.

PLAY IT SAFE

Any time you use an electric power tool around water there's a potential for injury or death. Never start the polishing process until you've taken some basic safety precautions:

- Use only a double-insulated tool.

- Don't use a tool whose cord is frayed or shows obvious signs of damage.

- Plug the tool into an outlet with a ground-fault circuit interrupter (GFCI) in the wall. These are now standard in bathrooms, kitchens, and other wet locations; you can also buy a portable GFCI outlet that plugs into a common three-prong *grounded* outlet; you can then use a regular extension cord. The circuitry senses even tiny imbalances in the current. In the event of an unintended ground, the GFCI shuts off power before it can hurt you.

- Test the circuit before you start by pressing the "test" button.

- Make sure the polisher is not high speed (more than 3,000 rpm).

Polishing concrete is a lot like sanding wood—you want the surface to be nice and even—not coarse in one area, fine in another. The trick is to work methodically so you make even passes over the entire surface with each grit pad.

Periodically, turn off the tool and squeegee the surface to check whether you've exposed the level of aggregate you want to show and that the surface appears even. The 50-grit and 100-grit disks will do almost all of the real cutting. Change disks only when you have exposed as much aggregate as you want to see. Repeat the process with the 200 and 400 grits, then stop and check for small holes. If you find holes, see "Adding the slurry" on the facing page. If you find few or none, continue working your way through the pads up to 1,500 grit for a very fine finish.

The finer grits primarily finish and polish the surface. They won't expose much more aggregate. There are no hard and fast rules as to how long you need to polish with each pad. It's mainly a matter of your personal taste. But clean off the surface regularly with the squeegee so you can see what you've done. And move on to the next grit only when you've removed all the swirl marks from the previous pad and when the surface appears smooth and uniform.

Polishing the hard-to-reach parts

Hand diamond pads are the best tools for finishing the corners and sides of the counter. They can be used on a wet or dry surface and, like disks, come in an array of grits. Hand pads allow you to reach into some tight spots that the power polisher can't get to. They also give you more control. However, unless you are extremely patient and persistent, don't expect to polish down to expose much aggregate with hand pads. Hand pads are suitable only for touching up (and removing small stains on finished countertops).

An orbital sander gets the job done, but it will take you twice as much time to polish as a water-fed professional polisher.

POLISHING BASICS

Here are some tips for getting an even surface on the countertop:

- Hold the polisher as flat as possible on the surface.
- Apply even pressure, and don't push too hard on the tool.
- Polish an area only as large as you can comfortably work on, then move on to the next area.
- Always work toward the water supply so there's ample water under the pad.
- Keep an eye on the power and water lines as you work.

After polishing, apply the slurry coat to fill in tiny holes and voids, if necessary.

Adding the slurry

Once you've finished polishing the entire surface (with a disk at least as fine as 400 grit), you'll have reached a fork in the road. The next step—adding a slurry coat to the counter and repolishing the surface—is optional. Slurry is a kind of filler that's used to repair surface blemishes. If the surface is porous after polishing or if there are holes or chip-outs, you should consider using slurry. On the other hand, if your concrete was well mixed and was the consistency of runny oatmeal and you did a good job with the vibrator, there's a fair chance your surface will be free from the holes caused by air bubbles trapped in the wet concrete. In which case, slurry would be unnecessary.

A slurry coat consists of a rapid-set, nonshrinking cement; pigment; and water. No sand is added, because we're trying to achieve a fine-textured fill that gets into the very smallest voids. You can make your own, but it's easier to use a prepackaged mix in which all the ingredients have been added in the right proportions (see Resources on p. 102).

Mixing and spreading the slurry

Dump the slurry mix into a container and then measure out and slowly add the prescribed amount of water to the dry mix. When it's just right, the mix should have a somewhat gelatinous consistency, something like toothpaste. Before applying the slurry, wet the concrete countertop thoroughly with water. Keep a spray bottle of water on hand to keep the concrete wet as you work.

When mixed, the slurry compound should have a thick, toothpaste-like consistency.

Apply the slurry

1 Rub it in Wearing gloves, grab a handful of slurry and press it onto the concrete surface. With the putty knife, start to spread the slurry back and forth over the surface, as if you were applying grout to tile. Really rub it into the concrete.

2 Fill and scrape Work quickly now, and be sure the slurry completely fills all of the holes in the surface. Scrape off the excess as you work. When the holes are filled, wipe the surface with a clean sponge or rag.

3 Let it cure When you're done, the surface should have a uniform appearance. At this point, allow the slurry to cure for 36 hours before polishing it.

The polished countertop is now ready for the next step in the process: sealing.

The repolish

Once the surface has dried, lightly polish with a 400-grit disk and water, just as you did initially. Concentrate on removing the dried slurry from the surface. Work your way up through the grits, and stop regularly to squeegee the surface and check your progress.

If the surface still shows divots where the slurry has receded into the holes, repeat the slurry, drying, and polishing process. Two coats are usually enough to fill all the holes. When the surface is flat and uniformly polished, you're done with this part of the process.

Once again, be patient. Before taking the next step, allow plenty of time (up to 48 hours) so the slurry in the concrete countertop can dry thoroughly.

The final pass

1 Repeat wet polish After the slurry is dry, polish lightly.

2 Keep checking Using a rubber squeegee, wipe the water and slurry residue from the concrete. Repeat as necessary.

Sealing

Concrete by nature is a porous material. Sealing and then waxing the countertop will help make it more resistant to stains, although it's nearly impossible to make concrete completely impervious to this problem.

Sealing the countertop first and then waxing the surface next brings out the natural luster of the concrete and the beauty of the inlays and aggregate. Waxing helps bring it to life. Periodic waxing also helps build more stain resistance into the surface.

Applying the sealer

Before you apply the sealer to the countertop, you have to make sure that the concrete surface is completely uncontaminated, free of all remnants of grinding, and dry to the touch. So, using a clean rag, thoroughly wet the surface with water and wipe down the countertop. With your bare hands, feel for grit or particles; if you feel anything, wash the countertop down until it's clean.

Wet, rub, and wipe down the concrete to remove grit before sealing.

For this last step in the finishing process, you'll need the following tools and materials.

Sealer and wax

Buffing wheel and pads

TOOLS AND MATERIALS

- Variable-speed grinder/polisher for buffing out the wax coat to a high sheen

- Buffing wheel and pads

- Latex gloves to protect your skin

- Ear protection while you're using the grinder/polisher

- Eye protection to prevent the sealer from splashing into your eyes

- Sealer to close off the pores in the concrete surface to prevent staining

- Water-based, food-safe wax for a final seal and polish on the concrete surface

- Clean sponges, rags, and/or towels

Our sealer requires that we thoroughly saturate the countertop with water before applying.

Choose the right sealer

There are two basic types of concrete sealers on the market. Each one has strengths and weaknesses. Whichever you choose, follow the specific instructions that come from the manufacturer.

TOPICAL SEALERS Topical sealers include epoxies, urethanes, and lacquer- and acrylic-based products. They sit on the surface of the countertop, essentially shrink-wrapping it in a plastic film. They are very effective against stains; but, unfortunately, they tend to scratch, peel, and fail over the long haul unless handled with utmost care.

Furthermore, these finishes must be completely stripped down with noxious chemicals if you want to refinish or repair the surface. Most of us don't want to face that burden. Finally, they don't look that great. They really take something away from the wonderfully tactile, earthy feeling of the concrete.

PENETRATING SEALERS The penetrating sealers include silicone, solvent-, and acrylic-based products. Of the three, the water-based acrylic sealers are the most food safe.

Many of these products have been formulated for the stone and marble industry, and they have had limited success in protecting concrete from acid stains such as from lemon juice, wine, and vinegar. But they are usually easily removed or can be renewed by simply applying new coats. They generally don't peel or scratch because they seep into the pores of the concrete. With a coat of wax, they maintain the natural look and feel of the concrete without a layer of artificiality.

With the best of these types, you can expect protection from staining and/or etching from acidic foods and liquids for a few hours to overnight before some damage occurs.

For the project shown here, I am using Pro-Formula sealer, a penetrating type. So the directions in the text are specific to this sealer.

Apply the sealer

1 Wipe it on Swirl the diluted sealer (50:50 water to sealer) onto the concrete in a circular motion, spreading the sealer thoroughly over the surface. Keep the sealer solution moving, covering surfaces that seem to absorb it for up to five minutes.

2 Saturate it Now saturate the surface with full-strength sealer, applying it in a circular pattern. Again, go over the countertop many times, and make sure there is complete coverage.

3 Remove and wipe clean Wipe off any excess with a clear rag. Do not allow the sealer to dry or it will leave streaks.

Apply the wax

1 **Apply wax** Using a clean cloth or towel, apply the wax to the concrete in small, manageable areas using a circular motion. Using another clean cloth, wipe off the excess wax as you go, area by area. Excess dry wax leaves unsightly streaks.

2 **Polish to shine** Let the wax dry for 2 minutes or 3 minutes, then polish immediately with a polisher, using a buffing wheel and a lamb's wool pad. Or work it by hand with just the lamb's wool pad. When you're finished the counter will have a beautiful, soft luster.

Buffed and polished, the concrete is now ready to be installed. If you're installing the countertop the same day, wait a day before subjecting the countertop to normal use.

Sealing the concrete

Once the countertop is thoroughly cleaned of debris, you can apply the sealer. The step-by-step directions apply *only* to the type of penetrating acrylic sealer I use in my operation. If you are using another brand of sealer, read the manufacturer's instructions, and, if possible, try it out on a small remnant piece of concrete.

No matter which brand of sealer you use, don't allow it to dry on the surface. Wiping it all down thoroughly before even a little bit of it has a chance to dry is essential to a smooth, no-streak finish. Also, wait a day and repeat the whole process with the full-strength sealer if you want maximum protection.

To apply the sealer, first dilute a small amount of the prepared sealer 50 percent with water, stir it well, and then sponge it over the entire surface. Saturate the surface with a wet-on-wet application, allowing the sealer to soak into the pores of the concrete and help bind the sealer to itself. Saturate and move the sealer around for up to 5 minutes. Follow the detailed steps, which are based on the directions found on the sealer that I use.

Applying the wax

After the last sealer coat has dried for several hours (two coats of this type of sealer is best with a day of drying in between), apply the wax with a clean cloth or towel. Depending on how much luster you want on your countertop, you may want to apply more than one coat of wax.

Let the wax dry for 2 minutes or 3 minutes, then wipe off any excess with another clean cloth. If the wax dries longer than about 3 minutes, it will be difficult to buff.

Installing

Your beautiful new concrete countertop is now complete—except for two important details. You still have to get it from the pour table where you created it to the bathroom vanity. Then you have to install it. Moving the countertop is a job for more than one person. As you've already discovered, concrete is heavy.

A countertop containing 3 cu. ft. of concrete will tip the scales at 400 lb.; and for all of its strength, the counter can be damaged in transit if it's allowed to bend under its own weight. It's especially vulnerable at the thin sections around the sink opening.

How to move it

With all this in mind, think ahead. Gather a few friends with strong backs, and remember that your new counter should be treated gently. It should be carried on edge so it won't bend, and your team should be careful not to twist it. Go over the procedure before you start. Take a look at your route through the house, get furniture and other obstacles out of the way, and talk about any potential trouble spots. Have a plan before you start. A dolly padded with carpeting can be a tremendous help in moving the countertop through the house.

Cabinets that need reinforcement

Some cabinets are strong enough to support the hundreds of pounds of a concrete countertop. Others need some reinforcement. In some cases, the reinforcement is a ¾-in. plywood back; in others, it's vertical or horizontal supports.

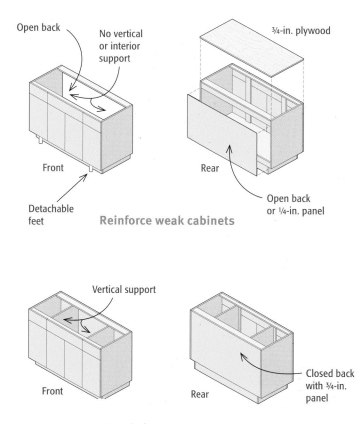

Reinforce weak cabinets

No reinforcement needed

nstallation requires very few tools, mainly human strength and careful planning. However, a few basic tools and materials are essential. Here's what you will need.

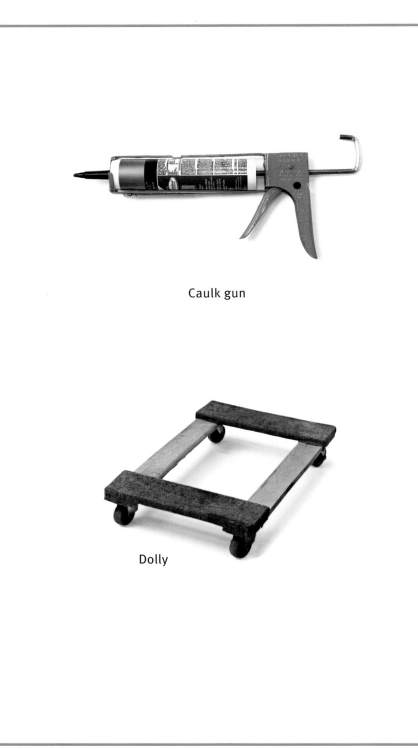

Caulk gun

Dolly

TOOLS AND MATERIALS

- Caulk gun and silicone caulk to seal the countertop to the substrate and the sink to the countertop

- Cordless drill with a ¼-in. masonry bit for pilot holes and for driving screws

- Dolly padded with carpeting for moving the countertop into the bathroom

- Shims to level the countertop

- ¼-in. plastic expansion anchors and metal clips to attach the sink flange to the bottom of the countertop

- Screws for holding the clips in place

With a strong-armed person on each end, gently move the countertop along on the padded dolly. Hold it vertical, like a piece of glass.

Beefing up a cabinet

Concrete is a very heavy material, and some cabinets aren't strong enough to support the weight without a little doctoring. Cabinet boxes should be made from ¾-in. particleboard or plywood—not only on the sides but also on the back. The top of the vanity can be covered with a sheet of ¾-in. plywood. Note that this will raise your countertop an additional ¾ in. If your new countertop is 2½ in. thick and you are using standard cabinets with standard kicks, make sure you are comfortable with the final countertop height. If necessary, you can take some height off of the kicks to reduce the overall height of the finished countertop.

If you don't want to add the plywood, install 6-in. by ¾-in. plywood rails across the front and the back of the cabinet to carry the weight.

If the cabinet came with light-duty plastic legs, discard them. The cabinet box should be supported by a kick frame made from ¾-in. plywood on the outside, glued and screwed together, and framed with 2×4s on edge.

If you cantilever one end of the counter—that is, if you intend for it to extend past the cabinet—make sure the overhang is no more than one third the length of the counter (or, if the counter is made in sections, no more than one third the length of that module).

Dry-fitting the countertop

The countertop will be held in place with silicone caulk. But before you break out the caulk gun, make sure the vanity has been adequately reinforced to carry the weight of the counter (see "Beefing up a cabinet" on p. 93).

Now it's time for a dry-fit—a bit of insurance to make sure you won't run into any surprises. Handling the countertop carefully, lower it onto the vanity slowly and gently. Watch the edges so they don't get chipped. Once the counter is in place, check to make sure it sits flat on the substrate. If the counter doesn't sit securely, insert shims (thin, tapered pieces of wood) between the countertop and the substrate so the counter doesn't rock or wobble. Take a look at the faucet knockout to make sure it's aligned with the plumbing, and check the overhang at the front of the cabinet.

If the hole for the sink hasn't already been cut out of the plywood on top of the vanity, now is the time to take care of that. With the countertop resting temporarily on top of the vanity, trace the sink opening onto the substrate then remove the countertop and set it aside. But before you cut out the hole, consider how you will mount the sink in the counter.

The ³⁄₄-in. plywood base has been routed out to create the recess for the undermount sink.

Installation

When assembled, the vanity should provide a sturdy foundation for the heavy concrete counter. Make sure the cabinet sits on a plywood or solid-wood kick (not plastic legs) and that the cabinet is strong.

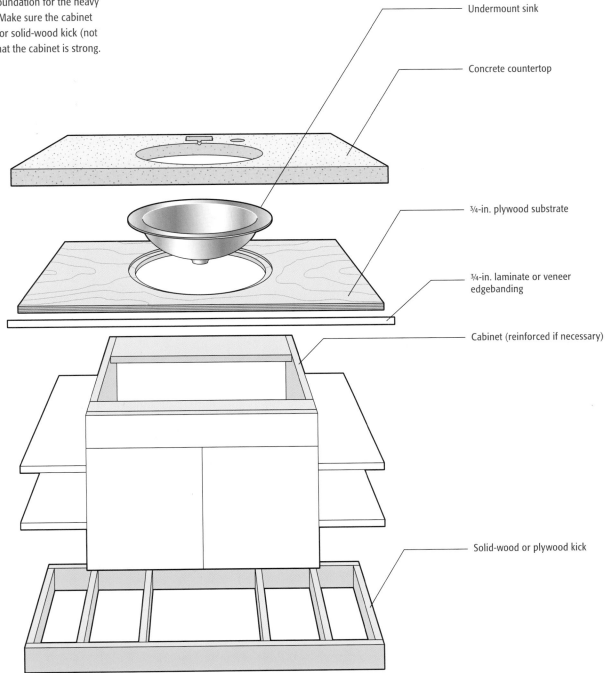

Undermount sink

Concrete countertop

¾-in. plywood substrate

¾-in. laminate or veneer edgebanding

Cabinet (reinforced if necessary)

Solid-wood or plywood kick

Getting ready for the sink

We're using an undermount sink for this project. It can be installed in two ways: using metal clips to attach the sink to the bottom of the counter or cutting a groove (properly called a *rabbet*) in the top of the plywood substrate to catch the rim of the sink.

Metal clips

When a countertop is wood, you can secure the clips (and the sink) by running screws right into the bottom of the counter. With concrete, however, that's not possible. You'll have to drill holes large enough for special concrete screws (Tapcon®) or insert anchors that in turn accept screws to secure the clips into the bottom of the counter.

To make sure you have enough room for the clips, the traced outline of the sink opening on the plywood should be enlarged slightly. Using one of the clips as a guide, determine how much of an allowance you'll need, then trace a slightly larger opening onto the plywood. Now cut the sink opening with a jigsaw. If you've already cut the hole in the top, make sure you've got enough room for the clips, and if not enlarge the hole to accommodate them.

A no-clip approach

The other approach, making a recess for the lip of the sink, is what we're doing here. You'll need to use a router with a bearing-guided rabbeting bit. The bit follows the opening in the plywood substrate and creates a small shelf or step for the sink. Don't try to cut the rabbet to its full depth all at once. Adjust the bit so it will take off only about ⅛ in. of material, and work your way around the opening. Then reset the bit, and do it again. The idea is to gradually sneak up on the right depth. When you're finished, the top of the sink lip should be even with the top of the plywood. Don't forget the clearance hole for the faucet.

Once those details have been taken care of it's time to install the counter. Apply a generous bead of caulk or construction adhesive to the plywood substrate and the rim of the sink, then lower the countertop on top of the vanity as carefully as you can. If any caulk oozes out, it can be cut away later with a single-edge razor.

Sink attachment

An undermount sink can be installed either by using metal clips that are attached with screws and screw anchors (below top) or by routing a groove in the edge of the plywood substrate deep enough to accommodate the lip of the sink (below bottom).

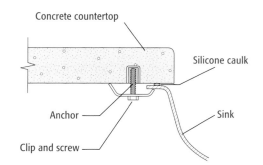

Concrete countertop

Silicone caulk

Anchor

Sink

Clip and screw

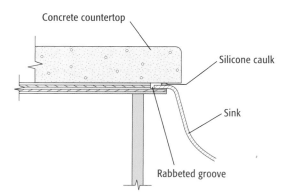

Concrete countertop

Silicone caulk

Sink

Rabbeted groove

Squeeze a generous, continuous bead of caulk (at least ¼ in. wide) around the middle of the sink flange. This will seal the sink to the underside of the countertop. Make sure that there are no gaps. Add more caulk if necessary.

For most countertops, continuous beads of silicone will act as an adhesive. In seismic zones, or any situation where the countertop could move, it is recommended to predrill holes into the underside of the countertop and use concrete screws (Tapcon) through the substrate or cabinet ledger in addition to silicone.

FAQs

At our website, chengconcrete.com, questions naturally come to us about process, construction, and maintenance of concrete countertops. Although we cannot solve every problem, many have simple solutions or explanations. Here are our responses to the most frequently asked questions.

How thin or thick can I cast my countertop?

At Cheng Design, we prefer thicker (from 2 in. to 3 in. thick, depending on the project) rather than thinner tops, as thicker tops not only allow you to include a bailing wire and rebar support system within the piece but give the countertop a substantial look and feel.

What are decorative aggregates?

Inside standard bagged concrete (like Sakrete 5000 Plus) is natural stone aggregate. When you polish the surface of your countertop, you are removing the "cream" layer to reveal these stones. To achieve a unique or custom look, supplement the natural aggregate with decorative aggregate.

How do I divide a large piece into sections?

A ⅛-in. strip of Plexiglas® at the depth of your countertop can be used as a divider in a large mold. Simply let in the Plexiglas to opposite sides of the mold front and back. A more sophisticated approach is to shape a thin sheet metal divide into a Z shape that acts as a "key" between the two sections.

How much work time do I have with the concrete mix while pouring?

Pro-Formula admixture mix achieves 85 percent strength in just 4 days. As a result, the work time with Pro-Formula is less than that of ordinary concrete. From mixing and pouring to screeding, you have approximately 30 minutes of work time. Work quickly.

How do I know when I've achieved the right concrete mix consistency?

A proper mix consistency looks and feels like runny oatmeal, especially during the time you are filling the mold. Too stiff a mix will result in many air pockets on the surface of the mold. With admixtures that contain water-reducing agents, you may add some more water just before filling the mold to make it more workable and fluid without giving up too much strength.

I just poured my countertop and it doesn't look like the exact color I thought I mixed. Why?

The actual final color will not be known until the countertop is fully cured, after approximately 28 days. Coloring concrete is an imperfect science. To help ensure consistent color on a project with multiple pours, buy all the concrete at the same time and pour on the same day. Also remember that bagged concrete is regionally produced, and the type and color of aggregates will vary from region to region.

How long do I wait before I can unmold my countertop?

After pouring a countertop, you can unmold it after 4 days, at which point the countertop is at 85 percent of full strength (approximately 4,250 psi).

How can I prevent cracks from forming in my concrete countertop?

Good mix design and proper curing are the keys to prevention. Countertop admixture products are designed to minimize cracking. They have micro-reinforcement fibers and water-reducer plasticizers (which lessen the amount of water needed in your concrete mix while maintaining its workability—another way to prevent a weak mix). Excess water in the mix weakens concrete. Do not disturb or move a curing countertop.

Is it possible to build a form around existing countertops and pour concrete directly on that surface?

This method is generally not recommended. It takes skill and experience with finishing wet concrete to make a surface flat and level.

Do I have to grind and polish my concrete countertop?

Not necessarily. If you like the results straight out of the mold, then you don't need to polish at all. To aggressively expose aggregate during polishing, start with 50-grit pads after 4 days to 5 days of curing time. To moderately expose the aggregate, start with a 100-grit or 200-grit pad. In either case, work up to 400 grit. Wait another 4 days to 6 days before doing the final polish.

How do I achieve a highly polished look?

You can achieve a high polish by carefully polishing with diamond polishing pads. Start with a 50-grit pad and then work your way through 100-grit, 200-grit, 400-grit, and 800-grit pads, finishing with a 1,500-grit pad. This is the process used by marble and granite fabricators.

When do I polish?

Polishing (800 grit and above) should wait until the piece is at least 10 days old but no more than 28 days. Concrete cured less than 10 days is still too soft to polish; concrete over a month old is very hard and requires a lot more effort and a lot of diamond pads.

Why do I need hand-finishing pads?

When you unmold a countertop, burrs and rough spots will appear on the edges and corners of your countertop. Use a hand diamond polishing pad to hit these spots. These pads are also great for touching up and removing stains.

What kind of grinder/polisher do I need?

Use a variable-speed polisher between 800 rpm and 3,000 rpm with a built-in water feed. Make sure it is double-insulated and comes with a ground-fault interrupter for safety. Do not use high-speed metal-angle grinders. These polishers can damage the pad holder or cause excessive wear to your diamond pads.

My countertops have a few small voids (created by trapped air). What is the best way to fill them?

Voids are best filled with a slurry coat, made of pure cement with either very fine sand or no sand at all.

How is concrete sealed?

The Pro-Formula sealer recommended in the book is a professional-grade sealer created from the latest water-based acrylic micro-emulsion technology. It creates a food-safe, non-yellowing barrier and penetrating sealer to protect and beautify. Regardless of the product, always follow the manufacturer's directions.

How many coats of wax do I apply? How long do I wait between coats?

For a brand-new countertop, we recommend two coats of wax. One coat of wax should be applied before installation, and the other coat after installation, to remove any marks and scuffs resulting from installation.

How do I clean my concrete countertop?

Washing your countertop with mild soap and water is the best method of cleaning. Be wary of cleansers and rough pads because they may have solvents and abrasives that can harm, scratch, or etch the surface of your countertop.

What routine maintenance is required to keep a nice finish on my concrete countertop? How often do I reapply the finishing wax?

We recommend that wax be reapplied every month. With each coat of wax, your countertop will develop a naturally protective coating. Many owners wax their countertops once a year or less, and some never do at all. Without upkeep and maintenance, your countertop will develop a patina and stain, but this will not affect the durability of the surface. Should it become necessary to restore the luster and remove stains from a concrete countertop, simply repolish it using the same method you used when polishing it after unmolding the counter.

Maintaining your countertop: some guidelines

- Don't use strong detergents or abrasive cleaners to clean the countertop. Instead, use a sponge and a diluted solution of mild soap and water.

- Wax the counter once a month with a food-grade, nonpetroleum-based wax, such as the Pro-Formula I use or a type of bee's wax used by stone countertop fabricators.

- Reseal the counter about once a year by treating the surface with a wax stripper, applying a penetrating sealer, then rewaxing and buffing.

- Etched spots, small stains, cup rings, and the like can be removed with small handheld 800-grit and 1,500-grit diamond sanding blocks (see Resources on p. 102). Just apply water to the spot and wet polish by hand. Start with 800 grit, and follow up with the 1,500. Reapply the sealer and wax.

- Sometimes it may be necessary to completely refinish a countertop that has been poorly maintained, subjected to unusually harsh treatment with food acids, abraded, cut on, or scratched. First, strip off any wax with a wax stripper. Then start wet polishing with the finest grit polishing pad that will cut through the scratches or stains (400 grit is a good place to start, but if there is severe damage, you may have to start at a courser 100 grit). Gradually work back up to 1,500-grit.

A countertop the size of our vanity project would require less than 2 hours to completely refurbish like new.

- If an accident should occur and a piece of concrete chips off, try to salvage the pieces. Use a two-part 5-minute clear epoxy to reattach them. If you actually lose a hunk of the concrete, you can use two-part light gray epoxy putty such as PC-7® plus a coloring pigment for repairs.

resources

on the web

- **www.chengconcrete.com**
  The author's complete on-line resource and web store for making concrete countertops. Specialty admixtures and mold-making supplies mentioned in the book can be found here. A listing of concrete contractors and designers is available.

- **www.concretedecor.net**
  Site of *Concrete Décor*™ magazine, a monthly trade journal of decorative concrete with up-to-date articles on countertop making, products, classes, equipment, flatwork, news, and more.

- **www.concreteideas.com**
  A decorative concrete database. Contractors and products are listed.

- **www.concretenetwork.com**
  A resource database for all concrete-related businesses and information. Products and classes offered by different countertop companies are provided.

training and professional support

- **Cheng Concrete Training Academy**
  The author's specialized 1-day, 3-day, and 5-day training programs in professional concrete countertops, kitchen and bath design for concrete, and the business of countertop making.
  www.chengconcrete.com
  510-849-3272 ext. 217

- **Amelia Concrete Fusion, Inc.**
  An Atlanta-based concrete furniture and countertop design/build shop that offers training and a full line of products.
  www.ameliaconcretefusion.com
  770-631-1881

- **Surface Studios**
  Workshops and programs for participants to gain hands-on experience in concrete countertop techniques and design principles.
  www.surfaceconcrete.com
  515-243-3450

supplies and materials

BAGGED CEMENT, CONCRETE ADMIXTURES, FINISHING TOOLS, AND MOLD-MAKING SUPPLIES

- **Sakrete**
  Their 5000 Plus bagged concrete (rated at 5,000 psi) is the best base mix for concrete countertops. Wide distribution, generally available across the country.
  www.sakrete.com

- **Basalite®**
  Bagged concrete and specialty concrete mixes.
  www.basalite.com

- **Cheng Concrete LLC**
  Pro-Formula countertop admixture; Pro-Form mold-making system; wet polishers, vibrators, polishing pads, sink and faucet knock-outs, ammonite fossils, decorative aggregates, and more.
  www.chengconcrete.com
  510-849-3272

- **Stegmeier LLC**
  A selection of concrete countertop edge forming systems for pour-in-place application.
  www.stegmeier.com
  800-382-5430 (tech line)

- **Polytek Development Corporation®**
  Liquid mold rubber for casting concrete.
  www.polytek.com
  800-858-5990

- **Smooth-On®**
  Liquid mold rubber for casting concrete.
  www.smooth-on.com
  800-762-0744

- **Alpha Professional Tools®**
  Wet polishers, dry polishers, grinding tools, polishing pads, and diamond pads.
  www.alpha-tools.com
  800-648-7229

- **Heritage Glass Inc.**
  Crushed glass for the terrazzo and concrete countertop industry.
  www.heritageglass.net
  435-563-5585

pigments and colorants

- **Blueconcrete.com**
  A division of Delta Performance Products LLC.
  Color, special effects, admixtures, aggregates, and custom color matching.
  www.blueconcrete.com
  770-464-2515

- **Interstar®**
  Quality pigments, admixture, and fiber manufacturer for the concrete industry and concrete countertops.
  www.interstar.ca
  800-567-1857

concrete vibrators

- **Vibco®**
  Professional table vibrators and controllers.
  www.vibco.com
  714-522-8088

- **Makita®**
  Cordless concrete vibrators perfect for the DIY project.
  www.makita.com
  800-462-5482

concrete mixers

- **Imer USA, Inc®**
  Reliable concrete mixers for both the amateur and the professional.
  www.imerusa.com
  800-275-5463

additional reading

- **Fu-Tung Cheng, *Concrete Countertops: Design, Forms, and Finishes for the New Kitchen and Bath*. (The Taunton Press, Inc., 2002).**
  The author's comprehensive first book on making concrete countertops for architects, designers, contractors, and concrete fabricators.

- **Fu-Tung Cheng, *Concrete at Home: Floors, Walls, Fireplaces, Countertops—Innovative Forms and Finishes*. (The Taunton Press, Inc., 2005).**

Designs and projects from the office of Cheng Design covering a wide range of highly custom, finished concrete work mainly in residential projects.

concrete countertop retail vendors

UNITED STATES

- **Adams Distributing**
  235 Main St.
  Ririe, ID 83443
  208-680-7848

- **Alta Paints and Coating**
  136 W. 3300th St.
  Salt Lake City, UT 84115-3704
  801-466-9625; 800-400-0427
  www.altapaints.com

- **Chicopee Masonry Supply**
  451 McKinstry Ave.
  Chicopee, MA 01020,
  413-534-4516
  www.cmsblock.com

- **Concrete Building Supply**
  1024 Military Turnpike
  Plattsburgh, NY 12901
  518-563-0700,
  www.concretebuildingsupply.com

- **Contractors Direct℠**
  143 Furniture Row
  Milford, CT 06460
  203-882-1650; 800-709-0002
  www.contractorsdirect.com

- **Granite Rock**
  540 W. Beach St.
  Watsonville, CA 95076
  831-768-2500
  www.graniterock.com

- **Ideal Tile℠, Kitchen & Bath Design Center**
  929 W. Broad St. No. 102
  Falls Church, VA 22046
  703-237-8400
  www.idealtile.biz

- **Integrity Concrete Designs**
  12969 Howell Prairie Rd.
  Gervais, OR 97026
  503-792-3145; 877-567-0567
  www.integrity-online.com

- **Northwest Trends**
  11315 E. Montgomery Dr.
  Spokane Valley, WA 99206
  509-921-9677

- **ONEX, Inc.**
  206 W. 30th St.
  Charlotte, NC 28206
  704-372-1560
  www.onexconcrete.com

- **Quad County Ready Mix**
  300 W. 12th Ave.
  Okawville, IL 62271
  618-243-5359
  www.quadcounty.com

- **Surface, LLC**
  321 S.W. 6th St.
  Des Moines, IA 50309
  515-208-3998
  www.surfaceconcrete.com

CANADA

- **B W Construction Products Ltd.**
  138 22nd Street North
  Lethbridge, AB, T1H 3R5
  403-327-2700,

- **Countercast Concrete Designs**
  No. 118, 6875 King George Hwy.
  Surrey, BC, V4A 6J3
  604-542-1322
  www.countercast.com

- **Industrial Plastics & Paints**
  3944 Quadra St.
  Victoria, BC, V8X 1J8
  250-727-3545
  www.ippnet.com

- **Invermere Hardware**
  9980 Arrow Rd.
  Invermere, BC, V0A 1K4
  250-342-6908
  www.invermerehardware.com

- **Concept Béton Design**
  205 Rue Des Entreprises
  Notre-Dame-des-Prairies,
  QC, J6E 7Y8
  450-755-1022
  www.conceptbetondesign.ca

- **Pantheon Decorative Concrete**
  89 Summerfield Close
  Airdrie, AB, T4B 2B9
  403-828-4581
  www.pantheonconcrete.com

- **Rowland Concrete Services**
  RR #2, 5595 Tottenham 4th Con
  Tottenham, ON, L0G 1N0
  905-936-2375
  www.rowlandconcrete.com

MEXICO

- **IVAN DE LA CRUZ**
  Prol. 5 De Mayo 919
  Monterrey, N. L. Mexico, C.P.
  64800
  81 81 90 43 54

index